PRACTICAL PARENTING
– AN IRISH SURVIVAL GUIDE

For my beautiful children and patient husband

Practical Parenting
An Irish Survival Guide

PAT REES

ashfield
PRESS

Published in 2006 by
ASHFIELD PRESS • DUBLIN • IRELAND

ISBN: 1901658-63-5

Typeset in 11 on 13 point Dante and Meta

Designed by SUSAN WAINE
Printed in Ireland by BETAPRINT LIMITED, DUBLIN

Contents

Introduction

H aving *advised parents* for many years and done many parenting workshops, I gradually saw the need for a book that was much more practical in content than the parenting books that were on offer. Yes, parenting courses and books on child psychology have their place and can help a great deal when developing as parents. However, when one is not reading a parenting book or actually doing a parenting course, how many of us really retain all the advice given for different situations that may arise? Courses really help a parent gain great skills and the confidence needed for parenting, but I felt that a parenting book should be *user-friendly*, so that a busy parent who did not know how to cope with a certain situation could just look up ideas on how to deal with that particular problem or situation, instead of having to wade through chapters looking for the pertinent paragraph.

Of course the way we bring up our children is a very personal matter and reflects a lot about the people we are. Many parents respond differently to any given situation. What I have tried to do, therefore, is to give several alternatives to each predicament or circumstance. One parent may opt for one idea while another may find his/her own solution. There are no definite correct answers in parenting, just different ways of approaching and solving a problem.

Parenting is much more than just responding to situations as they arise. If you look after yourself and be a good 'parent', if you like, to yourself, your body, your life and your well being, there is a good chance that your child will follow your example. The parent we are comes very much from within; that is why when one or both parents experience difficulties, it is often reflected in the children's behaviour.

However, this is not just a book about handling problems or difficult children. It contains all the most common questions parents have asked me over the years. Questions dealing with everyday life. From how to motivate a child to study or deal with a toddler having a tantrum, to what to do if you find your child smoking or simply how to curtail siblings who are constantly squabbling. Parenting should be a positive pleasure and because parents are from very varying backgrounds and cultures, and have varying abilities, the guide to parenting should be easy reading. Therefore following through on my user-friendly parenting guide, I also wanted to make sure that the book is sensible, easy to follow, practical but fun, and an enjoyable read, too.

Looking after other people's children is different from having your own. In this way, we parents are all beginners. How are we expected to know what to do or how to handle our children? They say that practice makes perfect, yet we must practise on our own children. Within this book are many questions and situations most parents will come across during their lifetime. The questions are to guide you and help you develop the skills necessary for good parenting. Adapt these questions to guide you in other situations that may arise. There are set formats you can follow for discussions or in conflict situations. Used well, they'll lead you to a deeper understanding of your children and develop more confidence in your parenting skills.

P.S. I have referred to the baby/child/young adult as 'she' throughout this book, not because I prefer girls to boys (I have both and love them equally) but to make the book easier to read! The advice can be applied to either sex.

COMPLAINTS

WE CAN'T GET A WORD OUT OF HIM

CHAPTER 1

0 to 5 The Early Years

MY CHILD WILL NOT STOP CRYING

Ways to soothe a crying child

A persistently crying child can make even a very relaxed parent feel desperate. It is only when we become the parent of a child that we really appreciate how disturbing and heart-rendering it can be to hear your own baby cry. That is how it should be, because babies' cries are their own powerful means of survival. Crying is their way of attracting your attention forcefully. Babies cry because they are trying to tell you something.

The first thing a parent should try to do is find out the cause of the crying, which can be easier said than done. It is like being lost in a foreign country and not knowing the language so we have to go by instinct sometimes. Below is a list of reasons why a child may cry. Go through them and see if any could apply to your baby; if none is found, go to the second list to see ways of settling your baby.

Reasons Baby May Be Crying

HUNGER – When was the last feed? Try another feed just in case, perhaps baby is having a growth spurt and needs extra feeds or it may be time to start on solid foods. Weaning can begin from around three to six months.

THIRSTY – Especially in the summer or if you have the central heating on at a warm temperature, baby may just need a drink of cooled boiled water or diluted fruit juice - try it and see.

WIND – To relieve baby's wind just sit her up straight and give her back a gentle pat so that any bubble of wind can come up naturally. If the burp still won't come try lying her across your knees, your hand under her tummy and the other hand gently rubbing her back, keeping her chest slightly higher than the rest of her body. If this does not work try different positions that may give relief for the baby, you may come up with a favourite for you both. Remember to wind baby at least once or twice during a bottle or a breast-feed.

DISCOMFORT – Is baby uncomfortable in position or is she too hot or too cold? Check her clothes are not too tight anywhere. Or that her nappy does not need changing. Is she wet, dirty or just sore?

FEEDING PROBLEMS – For example, if bottle-feeding, is the hole in the teat big enough for the milk to come through for her stage? Check the flow; it should be steadily dropping but not as big a flow. Too much or too little could cause wind and hunger problems for baby.

COMPANY – Does your baby just crave your company? She was very close to you for nine months and loves having you near. Is she just bored, over-tired and restless, unable to sleep? Then read the list below and try one.

REACTING TO YOU – Are you anxious, upset or unhappy in any way? Babies pick up our feelings very quickly.

Ways To Settle A Crying Baby

MAKE CONTACT – Give her a loving cuddle.

SWADDLE HER – Wrap her in a warm comfortable blanket that she is familiar with so she feels snug, secure and loved.

ROCK HER gently in your arms, a carriage or a swing or sling.

GRAB THE BUGGY AND WALK – movement and fresh air would be good for you both.

MASSAGE or stroke her abdomen or back gently.

SING, hum or talk gently to her. So you are a hopeless singer, turn on gentle music and dance slowly around the room, humming quietly. Perhaps you'll find she likes certain types of music. Sometimes babies even like the hum of vacuum cleaners or other machines, the noise soothes them.

TAKE A DRIVE – A ride in the car often helps, many parents try this one.

TAKE A BATH – Baby spends her first nine months in the womb water and some love the bath and find a big bath in warm water very calming and soothing. Pop her in and let her float gently well supported by you in the large bath.

A SOOTHER may comfort a fractious baby but do restrict its use or it will become a habit.

BABIES who cry at night may be better in your bed or in the cot beside your bed for comfort.

IF PERSISTENT crying continues without a cause showing itself, do see your public health nurse or G.P. It could be a medical problem or some other problem like COLIC.

IF PARENT IS DESPERATE – and it can happen to any parent when a child cries continually – put the baby in the cot, close the door and have a calming, slow-breathing break for your own sanity. Phone a friend, family or your partner and share how you feel. Alternatively, look up the number for help or support organisations like 'Parents Under Stress.' (see p. 168)

Finally, some babies cry for no apparent reason - they are just sensitive to change. All a parent can do is check out all of the above and then muster up all the patience you can, giving tender loving care to baby and yourself.

Some Tips to encourage a good sleeping pattern

A few very lucky parents may have babies that sleep from dusk to dawn, but for most of us the lack of a good night's sleep is one of the hardest things to cope with about being a new parent. Sleep deprivation is torture. It affects the whole family. So although each different baby has a different pattern of sleep and some need more than others, there are tried and tested techniques to help baby sleep, starting from the beginning, establishing a settled routine and sleeping pattern, then hints on how to cope with sleeping problems as or when they arrive. As with all my ideas pick out ones to suit your needs.

The Newborn Baby

Nearly all new-borns wake at night for one or two feeds – this is inevitable at the beginning. But it is important to create the right environment to encourage your child to sleep from the start.

To Create the Right Environment for Sleep

From the start, let baby know the difference between day and night, by feeding in a darkened room, avoiding noise, only changing baby if she has soiled her nappy. Avoid unnecessary light, noise or movement to encourage baby to go back to sleep.

Get into a nighttime routine and try to stay with it. For example, evening bath and feed at 6 to 8pm, feeding again just prior to you going to bed, to allow you get the maximum sleep time.

When feeding at night, some parents keep baby in their bed or their bedroom. This is OK if it suits the family. Others may prefer to keep baby in a separate room, so the baby is less disturbed, encouraging a longer sleep – the choice is yours. But pick the sleep pattern to suit you and do not initiate habits you are not going to want to continue. For example, if you rock the baby to sleep she will begin to expect it.

TEACH BABY TO SLEEP ALONE without intervention from you. That means if baby always falls asleep as she suckles or sucks on the bottle, she will want or need that to get her back to sleep if ever she wakes in the night. This will disturb you because she associates feeding with sleeping.

DEVICES THAT ENCOURAGE BABY TO SLEEP can include a tape recording of mother's soothing voice (made earlier). You can even buy tapes with womb water sounds on them. Or you could try any gentle music. Musical wind-up toys that play music and are fun to look at were very popular in my home.

RESIST THE URGE TO PICK UP YOUR BABY if she whimpers slightly. All babies make little sounds or cries through the night and rouse to certain levels of con-sciousness. Let them settle themselves naturally. However, never leave your baby crying alone for long periods of time, it could make them feel insecure.

3 To 6 Months Old

At this age, a pattern of sleeping should have emerged with baby recognising the difference between day and night. If this is not the case, make out a sleeping diary detailing when and how long she sleeps and when she feeds. Look for and encourage a pattern. Can you identify a reason for your baby's waking? Keep to a set routine.

Once a baby is 6 months old, gaining weight, and good at taking feeds in the day, there should be no need for nighttime feedings. If they have become a habit, try to keep night feeds down to a minimum, making them less important to the baby by making them boring, if necessary just giving water in the bottle or trying to settle her without a feed.

Remember that at this stage babies often cry for a little while as they settle down to sleep, even taking as long as 5 to 10 minutes before they settle. Resist the urge to go in if your child is just whimpering for attention.

The Older Child

Again, the older child loves a nighttime routine of being washed, teeth brushed, given a cuddle and kiss or bedtime story and perhaps a night-light put on. Encourage the use of a comfort toy or blanket that gives her security at bedtime.

DO NOT UNWIND TOO QUICKLY from activities and playing too quickly. Give a warning that bedtime is in 10 minutes and allow time to unwind. Milky drinks contain calcium, nature's natural tranquilliser, so give milky drinks towards bedtime.

BE CONSISTENT AND FIRM IN A KIND WAY when your 2-year old child starts testing bedtime rules, this will pass.

NIP IN THE BUD the 'I need water' tactic. Before you leave the room, ask your child if there is anything else she needs.

MY CHILD WON'T SLEEP – I'M EXHAUSTED   Q

Ideas To Help Parents Survive Sleeping Interruptions
BE PREPARED FOR NIGHT FEEDS AT FIRST. Understand your baby's sleep pattern and encourage it to change to suit you. If you have a problem, don't ignore it. Talk to someone and get help.

GET PARTNER INVOLVED IN NIGHT FEEDS or if breast-feeding, at least in changing baby in the night, which may help. If you are really tired, express the breast milk and let partner bottle-feed in another room so that mother can get a good night's sleep.

TAKE A NAP TOGETHER in the middle of the day. Sleep when baby sleeps – you need it. Have a regular break away from the baby. A new mother feels she is on call 24 hours around the clock. Accept offers of baby-sitting and have a nap, a relaxing bath or a walk in the fresh air.

DO THE MINIMUM OF HOUSEWORK, just the essentials.

Take any help offered and do not feel you have to cope alone.

CHANGE YOUR SLEEPING PATTERN to get the maximum benefit from sleeping. For example, go to bed with your baby or keep your baby up until you go to bed. Have an early night at least once a week. Try relaxation techniques to help you relax and sleep.

EAT REGULARLY AND WISELY, taking multi vitamins and minerals if necessary. It is easy to snack out and comfort eat at this time. Instead, eat small wholesome meals regularly.

TAKE REGULAR EXERCISE three times a week, even if it is walking in the fresh air with baby for 40 minutes.

MY TODDLER KEEPS WAKING AT NIGHT

Sleeping Problems That Can Occur

The older a child is, the easier it gets to reason with her. A reward system or star chart for going to bed might be established. A toddler could also be testing the limits and learning to rebel to see what happens.

MAKE SURE THERE IS NOTHING WRONG with her physically or that she is not frightened of anything in the room.

KEEP TO THE BEDTIME ROUTINE.

LOOK AT THE CHILD'S LIFE – if she has just started waking at night, check to see if it coincides with anything else, such as potty training, play school, emotional pressure at home or a new baby in the house. Sympathetically talk through any problems that she may be having.

LOOK AT THE CHILD'S DIET CAREFULLY – colourings and preservatives can affect some children's sleep pattern. Also eczema and allergies may cause irritation at night. Consult your GP.

USE INCENTIVES – I'll read you another story if you get into bed without making a fuss.

PRAISE YOUR CHILD when she goes to bed without making any fuss. We often forget this one!

IMPLEMENT A CHECKING ROUTINE if you feel the child is in a habit of just waking up. This is difficult to do and you should look hard at all the ideas already mentioned and see if any other solution could be tried. This checking method needs a lot of stamina, determination and support. The checking routine encourages the child to be able to fall back asleep on her own.

CHECKING ROUTINE

- If child begins to cry, go in and reassure with a kindly but firm manner. Tuck her in to show you mean it and say she is not going to be picked up. It is sleep time.
- Leave the room but if she continues to cry stay near and go in after 5 minutes and settle again, repeating that it's sleep time, not picking up time, with a gentle but firm voice to show you mean business.
- Repeat this procedure if she continues to cry, going in regularly and reassuring her but letting her know it's bedtime, until she finally settles.
- This process is repeated each night and hopefully after 3 or 4 nights the child will realise that she is crying without any success and so will settle herself down to sleep without crying.

These frequent visits reassure your child that all is well. But firmness and consistency are a must, so go forward knowing you are doing the right thing. Your child needs a healthy sleeping pattern to thrive.

Finally, I know when you are suffering from lack of sleep the world can seem very negative. Don't be hard on yourself – many us have walked the floorboards with crying children before you. There is light at the end of the tunnel; your child will sleep all night at some stage.

MY BABY HAS COLIC, WHAT SHOULD I DO?

Information On The Management Of Colic

Colic is a particularly distressing condition for both baby and parents. It occurs in many infants and shows itself in persistent and forceful crying for long periods of time, with the result that the parents of a baby with colic can end up frustrated and exhausted. The term colic can cause disagreement because it is not fully understood, and the treatments vary depending what originally causes the colic.

What is colic and what is just crying? The term colic is usually applied when an apparently healthy infant cries for more than an hour or two at a stretch and this crying happens regularly. It is also applied when the baby cannot be comforted by cuddling or feeding etc. but seems to be in pain, drawing up her little legs in distress.

Often colic occurs when the baby is between 3 weeks to 3 months old, and in the early evenings. However it can occur at other times and stages.

What Could Be Wrong?

SEVERE WIND – baby could just have severe wind. This can

be caused by many things such as under feeding, over feeding, the hole in the teat being too small or too big, poor positioning on the breast. Normally when a baby is winded the air comes up as a burp. Sometimes, however, the consistency of the food in the stomach alters and the air gets trapped and is passed to the gut = colic.

INTOLERANCE – allergy to cows' milk should be investigated. It could also be lactose intolerance, in which case Lactaid can be added to the baby's formula, as this is very effective in relieving the colic.

CHECK OUT THE INFANT WITH YOUR GP in case there is any underlying medical problem. The baby suffering from colic should not have a temperature or be vomiting, and will appear healthy in all other ways.

STAY CALM AND RELAXED – the baby can sometimes pick up the tension or stress on the mother's part. However, this is difficult when a baby is screaming her head off. Do your best and make sure you get a break from the crying. Don't be hard on yourself; colic can happen to any baby, it is no one's fault. I have found that many mothers blame themselves. Please don't, it is soul destroying enough to care for a crying baby.

HUNGER – at times a colicky baby is really just a hungry one with a big appetite. At around 3-6 months, baby may need to have solid food introduced to keep her satisfied.

OTHER REMEDIES that could be tried are the traditional gripe water. Its efficacy is debatable, but it can help. Herbal teas like fennel have been known to soothe a colicky baby. You can buy colic drops in a pharmacy to break down the large wind bubbles into smaller bubbles that are supposedly expelled more easily by the baby.

OESOPHAGEAL REFLUX, which gives baby heartburn, may be the cause of the colic. Keeping the baby in the upright position after feeding can help to relieve this, as it is when the baby is laid down that the stomach contents slip into the oesophagus, causing the burning and pain. Carrying baby in a sling after meals could prevent this and aid winding, too. Introducing solid food or thickening food would also make it less likely to rise up.

HOW DO I CHILDPROOF MY HOME?

Preventing Accidents In The Home
Until we have children, we probably don't realise there are so many lethal appliances or dangerous things in our home. Accidents happen and we can never completely protect our children. However, we can do a lot to prevent accidents from occurring. We can provide a safe environment and point out danger areas. Fit safety devices and teach our children ways of keeping safe.

TIMES TO PLAY IT SAFE

0 - 6 Months
CHANGING TIMES – use a stable surface at a convenient height. Always keep one hand on the baby. Have all you need for changing her near at hand.

BATH TIMES – use a small plastic tub on a sturdy stand in a big bath or on a covered floor, or use a rubber mat inside a big bath. Keep baby from taps, run cold water first. Never leave baby alone, even for a second.

FEEDING TIMES – be sure all bottles, teats etc. are thoroughly sterilised for the first 6 months. Throw away any unfinished bottles because germs breed in warm milk. Don't leave an infant alone whilst eating; she can easily choke. When weaning, sieve foods carefully in early days to prevent choking on lumps. Always use safety harness in high chair when feeding.

SLEEP TIMES – no pillow for babies. Place Moses basket on stand or floor, not on the bed or sofa. Baby nests are not for sleeping in. Take off any plastic on baby mattress. Use a cat net for outdoor naps, or indoors if you have cats near by. All baby's nightclothes should be fire resistant.

PLAY TIMES – be careful of bouncing chairs. Even a very young baby can bounce a chair off a counter, so it is safer to keep it on the floor. Check toys for any bits that could break off. Keep a watchful eye on toddlers 'playing' with baby – they can be rough. Baby walkers are fun but can cause lots of accidents; keep them under observation.

OPEN AREAS – the hallway, stairs and landings of a home are where serious accidents can occur. Keep these areas free from toys and rugs that could be slipped on. It's sometimes better to let children go barefoot rather than to slip on socks. Make sure these areas are well lit, even at night, so a little one cannot tumble in the dark.

CRAWL – before your child can crawl, get down on all fours and crawl around your home so that you can see any dangers for yourself and correct them. Sharp corners on tables or low-lying ornaments may become obvious. This the age of curiosity – can they get these? Fit in it? They'll love to exper-iment and investigate.

STAIRWAY – fit safety barrier or gates, one for the top of the stairs and one for the bottom. Make sure the banisters are secure and have bars close enough together so a little head cannot get stuck in between them. Do not use horizontal bars, as they can be used as ladders.

GLASS – be careful of glass. Avoid it at the bottom of stairs or in doors. If you do have it, ensure it is safety glass that has been toughened. Alternatively, place a safety film over the glass for temporary safety – this can be purchased in many nursery shops.

DOORS – doors are usually our first defence against the world outside. Make sure your front and back door can be secured with locks. A high bolt out of the reach of a young child on a chair is a good investment. Teach a child never to open the door to a stranger. Do not allow a child under 5 to answer the door. Teach a child the dangers of doors, for example not to play near a closed door that can open unexpectedly and not to put fingers near to the hinge or opening.

FIRE – keep a guard up at all times. Don't put intriguing, mysterious items on the mantelpiece that a curious child may want to investigate. Make sure clothing and upholstery fabrics are fire-retardant. Teach a child in simple words the danger of fire and hot things.

ELECTRIC EQUIPMENT – ensure that these are all wired correctly and do not over-load. Tidy away all flexes from prying little hands. Teach your children the danger of playing with electric sockets; keep unused sockets protected by plastic safety covers.

CHAIRS – invest in a five-point harness and use it in all chairs, seats or prams. Do not leave your child unattended in a high chair – a harness will not help her if she choking. Keep the high chair a little away from the table or the toddler may be able to push it over by kicking the table. Do not put a baby in a bouncing chair on a work surface; it is easy for her to bounce it off and fall, causing injury.

KITCHEN – this is a dangerous place. Appliances with flexes that can be pulled, blenders and toasters have spaces where little fingers can fit. So leave work tops uncluttered and put appliances away when not in use. Keep washing machine and dishwasher doors shut. Always unplug tumble dryers when not in use. Keep dangerous fluids or household chemicals in locked cupboards. Keep sharp objects out of reach. Invest in safety catches for cupboards and drawers, and tape if necessary. All parts of a cooker are dangerous. Don't leave panhandles sticking out. Never leave pans unattended, whoever phones or calls. Use the back rings first and switch cooker off at the wall when not in use. Explain the dangers of the cooker at an early age. Keep a fire blanket in the kitchen for emergencies and fit a smoke alarm at a carefully thought-out area.

BATHS – these are fun if you just keep to the rules. I have mentioned some of these before but it's worth repeating. A child can drown in only a few inches of water. The water can scald if too hot. Slippery baths can cause falls. So never leave young children alone in the bath. Pour the cold water in first, then hot, and test temperature with your elbow. Use a non-slip mat and sit your child away from the taps.

BEDROOM – make your child's bedroom as safe a place as possible. Moses baskets and cribs should not be used once a baby can roll over. Also, once they can get out of the cot they'll investigate every corner. Check the cot for safety regulations. Do not place cot near curtains or blinds – the cords can strangle. Do not use a pillow, a duvet or a cot bumper for a child under 12 months old. Bunk beds can be dangerous for children of any age but especially those under 6 years old age.

WINDOWS – these are highly dangerous. Do not open the bottom sash; fit catches that allow ventilation but do not allow the window to be opened too much. Fit security locks but keep the key in a safe place where people can have access in case of fire. Do not leave chairs etc. under windows that a child can climb onto.

GARDENING GUIDELINES – all children need to have access to fresh air and space to exercise. Children should be well supervised outdoors when young. Gates and fences are an escape route so check if locked. All sharp garden implements or gardening chemicals etc. should be kept in a locked cupboard. Garden ponds and paddling pools of any description are a danger, even if just a few inches deep. Observe whilst on swings etc. Parasites from animal droppings can cause infection, so 'scoop up poops' regularly. Cover sandpit so that animals can't foul it. Avoid having poisonous plants in your garden. Teach general safety like not to run in front of swing, not to push if on a climbing frame, not to eat seeds or berries from any garden.

Health Safety – Teach And Train
Some sickness is a part of life. But some can be prevented or at least discouraged. These tips will not keep your family disease-free but are worth doing to give your child a healthy edge.

BREAST FEED – mother's milk is full of infection-fighting antibodies.

FREQUENT HANDWASHING – make this a family rule.

TEETH BRUSHING – encourage this after each meal and before bed. Visit the dentist regularly.

COUGHING – encourage children to cough into their handkerchief or shoulder; it is much less likely to spread disease than coughing germs into hands.

YES OR GO AREAS – have these in different rooms in the

house, it makes life easier. For example, allow access to a lower cupboard that is full of unbreakable things that they can play with.

SHARP THINGS – teach older children the dangers of scissors, pencils, pen tops and sharp bitty toys, and how to use them.

SMOKING – tell your children early about the horrific dangers of smoking cigarettes.

SAFETY WARNINGS – repetition of routine safety warnings and dangers develops automatic safety habits in children. Simply say nicely, 'Watch your fingers and toes', or 'Hot radiator.'

HEALTHY EXAMPLES – remember that children learn by example, so set a healthy one by eating wisely and exercising regularly.

Safety Items Checklist

A must – smoke detector, fireguard, harness (five point) and window locks.

Necessary – stair gate, safety glass or film, curly flexes or guards in kitchen.

Important – bathmat, doorstops, socket covers, oven guard.

Optional safety extras – catches for cupboards, dishwasher, fridge and washing machine, thermometers for nursery bath and fridge.

Q

MY TODDLER HAS TANTRUMS NEARLY EVERY SECOND DAY – WHAT SHOULD I DO?

Taming Toddler Tantrums

I know that it can be upsetting and aggravating, not to mention embarrassing, when you are out in public and your darling child seems to turn into a monster. It can often happen when we parents are tired or under stress, too.

So I know it is easy to read that it is a toddler's way of saying, 'Help! I am overwhelmed, over-tired and can't cope,' but in reality it is very difficult to deal with a toddler having a tantrum.

Yet how we handle these tantrums is very important because we can actually reduce their frequency and limit the tantrum stage if we just handle them in the correct way. Toddlers can be so wonderful and loving most of the time. However, they can also display a wide range of antisocial, unpleasant behaviour all at the same time in a tantrum.

Tantrums tend to start when a toddler is around 2-years old and gradually reduce as the child gets older, hopefully stopping altogether when about 5 years. However, it is not considered normal behaviour for a 2-year old to have two tantrums daily – heaven forbid! So although tantrums are normal at this phase, how we parents handle the tantrums can help it pass more quickly and as peacefully as possible.

Firstly, watch out for triggers!

To help you understand why a child had a tantrum, ask yourself why it happened.

OVERTIRED – avoid outings with a tired toddler if you can. Keep to regular sleep habits and nap routines to prevent this.

MEALTIMES – can be dangerous for tantrum battles. Do not be provoked, offer the food and leave it for her to eat. She could be testing you to see how much she can get away with or how to exert her will over yours. If she refuses to eat, take it away calmly but no snacking. Offer the food again later when the child is really hungry.

DRESSING – can be frustrating for everyone. Allow plenty of time and within reason allow her to choose. Give her something to look forward to once she is dressed; then she may be more co-operative.

TOILET TRAINING – may become stressful, so take it slow and easy or have a rest. Stay calm and start late; making it a game is best.

PARTY TIMES – following a fun event like a party or outing is a common time for tantrums. She's tired and may have consumed lots of sweet things; coloured sweets in particular make little ones hyper.

FRUSTRATIONS – a number of small frustrations may have occurred in her little life and she suddenly bubbles over with emotion and gets out of control. Or she just may want her own way!

HUNGER – a hungry child is an unreasonable child, so don't let her get overly hungry. Toddlers prefer small meals frequently, rather than two big ones.

ALLERGIES – allergies and sensitivities to certain foods can cause unreasonable or hyper behaviour. If you suspect this, discuss it with your GP.

What To Do If A Tantrum Occurs
•   Firstly, try to stay calm and remember that she is

overwhelmed and out of control so you, the adult, must try to stay in control and teach *by example.*

- Distract her prior to boiling point if you can, produce a toy, talk about a future outing, anything to distract.
- Give a warning: 'If you do not stop that we will go home / I'll leave the room / stand you in the corner.' Or if you prefer the light-hearted approach, say, 'Oh what a face you are pulling. You'll frighten everybody.'

If she is totally out of control:

- Isolate her and physically hold her firmly, facing away from you and whisper comforting things in her ear (if you can manage it). Or hold her in a chair facing the wall or put her somewhere safe alone for a while to calm down (it may be good for you to have some breathing space, too).
- Once she has calmed down, talk about what happened. If the reason for the tantrum needs a punishment, this might be 'time out' from a favourite activity or not watching a cartoon. Give an explanation why.
- Teach other ways of expressing anger by doing some form of exercise, running, punching a pillow. Or by using words, saying in words why you are angry! Give her time and attention to explain how she feels and praise good behaviour, ignoring bold behaviour as much as you reasonably can.
- Start a reward or star chart for good behaviour, focusing on good behaviour rather than bold behaviour.
- Give a good example by not reacting badly to a tantrum by shouting and being out of control.
- Be observant. Children with communication difficulties may have more tantrums because they get frustrated. Excessive tantrums could be a sign of a problem like a slight hearing impairment, language difficulties or slow development. If you suspect there may be a problem, talk to your GP.
- Breath holding or vomiting could be part of the more

severe tantrum. The child is usually doing it for attention so just calmly clear away the vomit without comment. If holding her breath, it looks very worrying to the distracted parent but after a few seconds she will automatically breathe again. The less fuss made about these antics, the fewer times the child will use it. If it works she will repeat it again.

Tantrums are difficult for even the calmest of parents. It often helps to talk to other parents, especially mothers of young children. It will reassure you that yours is not the only little loved one who turns into a monster at times and that you are not the only parent who feels like having a tantrum too, at times.

The Tantrum Checklist
- Be loving but firm.
- Avoid triggers.
- Give a warning.
- Stay calm and in control.
- Be consistent.
- Be strong and positive in your approach.
- Be firm and mean what you say.
- Praise good behaviour and ignore bad.
- Be realistic in your expectations.
- Keep your sense of humour – you'd laugh if you were a fly on the wall watching!

MY CHILD IS NOT TALKING YET – HOW CAN I ENCOURAGE HER TO TALK?

Giving Your Child An Edge In The Talking Department
Children learn to speak by imitating what they hear. If they hear Irish they speak Irish, if they hear English they speak

English and so on. So your baby must hear you and you must speak to your baby. Young babies listen to sounds as well as words. They learn that the noise of tap water running means they are going to have a lovely bath. Playing a tune from the toy over her cot indicates sleep time.

Children learn to talk at different rates and parents often worry about speech development. The truth is we help our children to talk from their birth and even before. Speech does not just come out of the blue. Her first word has been coming for a long time. She listens, takes it all in and then tries to 'ahh' or 'oh' or respond in any way she can.

Here are a few guidelines on how to know what to expect, how to encourage speech, and what to do if something is worrying you.

What to Expect

1 YEAR – babies are making various babbling sounds babbling and understanding lots of words. Perhaps they can even say a few, and follow simple instructions like, 'Wave bye bye.'

1 to 2 YEARS – in general most infants say their first words and learn to understand much more.

From 2 YEARS – the words start to be put together. Firstly in twos ('all gone') and then three together ('mummy gone work').

From 3 YEARS – four word sentences are put together and a rapid growth of vocabulary develops. She will add the proper endings like play*ed* or car*s* and the questions will come fast and furious.

AT 4 YEARS – she should be able to understand everything you say, except complicated sentences or words. She will have a vocabulary of 1,500 words.

AT 5 YEARS – her vocabulary will blossom to thousands of words and her grammar will be improving all the time. She'll be starting to read and make up her own stories.

Encouraging Speech

There is much evidence that you can talk to your baby whilst she is still *in utero* prior to her birth and she will respond, particularly to certain sounds like familiar music played regularly throughout pregnancy. Describe, sing, talk and read to your baby. Repeat nursery rhymes, play games like 'round and round the garden'. Explain what you are doing in everyday life. 'We are going to change your nappy now.' 'Let's go out into the garden, shall we?' Babies should be exposed to language at every opportunity.

ONE-TO-ONE – watching T.V. or listening to a stereo does not have the same effect as your one-to-one human input.

CHAT – when you speak to baby, wait for answer. At first it may just be an answering smile or burp. Gradually though, she'll be 'going' or babbling back to you. Have a chat.

BABY TALK – try not to use too much baby talk, though a little is hard to resist sometimes.

ATTENTION – let her know that you love speaking with her. She'll be delighted with your attention.

BOOKS – read books with her from the beginning. The rule of thumb is that a story should match her level of development, so books should have lots of nice pictures in them at the start, with lots of repetition, sight, sounds, rhyme and actions included.

UNDERSTANDING – remember that she will always understand much more than she can speak.

READING TIME – develop a special reading time, when you hold her close on your knee and read.

BONDING – sharing the love of books together is a bonding, loving, close thing, which should be done together regularly.

Common Worries
Talking is a complicated business and there are many little hiccups that a child may have. Thankfully many resolve themselves. Here are some difficulties a child may encounter.

Late Talkers
NOISES – as long as your child seems to understand what you say, there is probably nothing to worry about. However, if an infant is not making knowing noises by 1 year or not talking by 2 years, your GP needs to check her out and perhaps refer you to a speech therapist.

HEARING LOSS – this can affect speech. If in doubt, go to your GP, and a hearing test should be done. Glue ear and lots of colds can cause speech delay because of the effect on hearing; it is like hearing underwater.

INSTRUCTIONS – if she cannot follow simple instructions by the age of 2½, this should be investigated.

UNDERSTANDING – consult your GP if other people in or outside the family circle have difficulty understanding what she is saying when she's 4 years old.

HESITANCY – seek help if she is still hesitant, halting or unsure of her speech at 5 years and appears to be behind others of her age.

INSTINCT – if you are unhappy about her speech for any reason, talk to someone. I feel parents have an instinctive feeling if something does not seem right. Follow any instinct you have but do not show any concern to your child or you may make her nervous about speaking.

Stammering

This is quite a common occurrence. In fact, 1 in 3 children stumble, hesitate and repeat themselves mid-sentence. Stammering usually resolves itself, so do nothing apart from staying relaxed and calm, giving her plenty of time to speak. Do not speak for her or tease her or point it out. Let her know that you love speaking with her, give her space and it should resolve itself in a matter of months.

Seek help if...
- Stammering is in the family.
- If the stammering is very severe and goes on longer than a month.
- If it makes her or you anxious or if it interferes with her relationships.

Bad pronunciation

As a child gets older there can be problems with pronunciation or grammatical errors. These can be part of normal development, for example problems with the endings of words, *ca* instead of *cat*. She may say cutely *puddy ca*, which is fine when very young but should improve with age. Three year olds may use *p* or *b* instead of *f* or *th*. Some children as old as 4 or 5 years may still have difficulties with *r*, *w* and *y*. This is OK and it is best not to correct, but perhaps you could repeat the word correctly in your reply. Grammatical errors are a normal part of growing up, too, like, '*Me eated my dinner*'. Just speak correctly yourself and she'll get it eventually.

Seek help if...
- You are having difficulties understanding her at 3 years – no one understands a child's speech better than her parents.

- Her pronunciation seems to be deteriorating instead of improving.
- You, a teacher or anyone else suspects hearing problems.
- You and others cannot understand her when she is 4 years old.
- She is experiencing difficulties that are obvious at 5 years.

Language is so important not just because it can cause serious learning problems but also because a child can lose confidence if people do not understand what she is trying to say. Her writing, reading and all schoolwork could be effected. So if you suspect a problem, don't delay. *Talk* to your GP, public health nurse, teacher or speech therapist.

I NEED TO GO TO WORK - WHO WILL LOOK AFTER MY BABY?

Child Care Choices

Sometimes mothers choose to return to work after having a baby. Unfortunately some mothers do not have the choice and need to work for financial necessity. Whatever the reason, when you work outside the home you need someone to care for your child. There are advantages and disadvantages in a mother/father staying at home and going to work.

Advantages Of Returning To Work

For You...

- Regular income
- Keeping the status you had prior to becoming a parent.
- Keeping job skills, so a better chance in developing your career further.
- Giving you a separate identity from your role in the home.

- Keeping up working contact and friends.
- Giving a firm definite structure to your daily routine.

For Your Baby...
- If mother isn't suited to staying at home, baby will have a happier mother.
- Baby has the opportunity to develop relationships with others, including carers and other children, if in a nursery or with another family.
- Baby will learn to mix at an early age.

For The Family...
- Less financial strain hopefully, although there will be childcare costs.
- Sharing in the parenting of new baby.
- Having a more balanced relationship with partner.

Disadvantages Of Returning To Work

For You...
- If you are a parent who thrives at home and loves baby care, you could be heart-broken leaving your little one and feel guilty.
- Problems balancing demands at home and work could cause strain.
- You may miss her first few steps, smile, tooth etc.
- A close network of parents, friends, group outings and relationships can develop within a parenting circle, leading to friendships that may last a lifetime for both you and the baby. You may miss out on this.
- Childcare costs plus tax may mean you are practically working for nothing, with all the effort involved.

For Your Baby...
- May miss her parents, the ones closest to her in the whole world.

- She may be difficult to get to sleep at night because she wants to be with you longer.
- She may suffer from separation anxieties.
- It may be difficult to find just the right person to care for her.

For The Family...
- Could get stressed and stretched because the parents work long hours, then have to divide the time left between all the children, home chores etc., with less of a social life.
- Problems may occur if anyone becomes sick, carer or family.

There is no perfect solution – we all do the best we can under the circumstances given to us. So here are some hints to make returning to work go smoothly.

Practicalities
TIMING – time your return to work carefully to avoid any additional stress. Do not do it if child is sick or at a difficult stage or you are under extra strain, like moving house for example.

CHILDCARER – think carefully about who you would like to care for your baby. The choices are usually family, friends, half day swaps with other parents, au pair, live-in student, child-minder; the venue can be their home or yours, a nursery, crèche. These choices depend on whether you want one-to-one care or other children to be around, if you want help with the housework, and so on. Write a list of your needs.

THINGS TO ASK A CHILDMINDER!

- Is s/he single, married, boyfriend/girlfriend, engaged?
- A smoker?
- What she plans for a typical day with your child?

- How safety conscious is she, has she any first aid, what would she do if...?
- Can she drive?
- Personal health details.
- Explain truthfully what you expect from her, check if is she happy with that.
- What references has she? Contact them.
- What are her long term plans?
- Discuss salaries, sickness and holiday arrangements.
- Give her a chance to ask questions, meet baby and look around.
- Go by instinct – do you like her, feel you can trust her? Is she warm with the baby?

Do not make an immediate decision. Allow yourselves a day to think about it, then decide but remember that good minders are generally snapped up quickly. Make a written contract together.

CHOOSING A CRÈCHE OR PLAYGROUP

Practicalities

- Choose one near your home for practical reasons.
- Is there a staff of warm, loving people trained to work with children?
- What is the child to adult ratio? It is recommended that there should be 1 trained minder for every 3 babies, 1 per 6 toddlers and 1 per 12 children. Is it is same staff daily? Continuity is important. Is the place big enough for the number of children being cared for?
- Is it a clean, safe environment? Are toys readily available? Are there low, accessible shelves with books? Is there other equipment, such as jigsaws and paints, in evidence? Is there access to the outdoors, gardens?
- Is there a structured routine each day, offering stimulation, rest, story time and outings? What happens if a child is unwell?

- Are lunches available and special needs catered for?
- Is the place fully insured? Can you see the policy and any diplomas for staff?
- Are you made to feel welcome?
- Are the children there and your child treated with tenderness? Do the children look relaxed and happy?

Your local Social Service Board may have a list of the childcare groups and services available near you.

Your Child

- Prepare your child for the nursery/play group by talking to her about what is going to happen there. Visit it together beforehand, look around and perhaps leave her for a short time, initially.
- Once you start, keep it up so she gets used to the regularity.
- Talk about how she got on with the helpers.
- Talk about what she did during her day; she may show you new skills she has learnt.
- Be prepared for the odd cry or upset, especially as you drop her off in the morning.

MY LITTLE GIRL IS SUCH A FUSSY EATER, HOW CAN I TEMPT HER?

DEALING WITH EATING PROBLEMS

Refusing to eat, eating the wrong foods or being a very finicky eater are common problems, especially from about 18 months to 5 years old. Parents may find that meal times can become battlegrounds or a battle of wits. But this need not be the case. Regular family meals are important because they are a chance for the family to talk, share, discuss and generally enjoy each other's company. Learning to join in with this is part of our child's social development. That is why the fussy eater can make meal times miserable for everyone concerned.

Feeding is known to be one of the biggest concerns for parents of young children. But we must remember one vital point – YOUNG CHILDREN WILL NEVER STARVE THEMSELVES whilst they have access to wholesome food. So if they are sickly and go off food for a time, do not worry overly, their appetite will return.

Common Difficulties Experienced

Tempting the Fussy Eater
DISGUISE – vegetables in home made gravies, soups and puréed sauces. Vegetables covered in cheese or cooked with a little honey in the water may be accepted more readily.
MILK SHAKES – can disguise blended fruit purée or fruit yoghurt.
SNACKS – try bite-sized dates, fruit slices or dried apricots.
COMPANY – toddlers love company, so let her sit in on a big family meal if she eats her dinner.
VEGETABLES – don't insist on cooked vegetables, many toddlers love to chew on raw veggies like carrots sticks.
SMALL BUT OFTEN – be prepared to give small meals more frequently, some infants like to eat like this. Make it easy on yourself, for example a peanut butter sandwich, boiled egg with toast, cheese crackers plus cheese and slices of apple. Offer her a little of the meal that you are giving the rest of the family sometimes.

Food Refusal
Food refusal is often linked with food fads. The main thing is to stay relaxed and not allow her to manipulate you with food, thus speeding up the day when she will grow out of it.

What To Do?
• Do not become angry and emotional.

- Accept that missing the odd meal will not harm her.
- Never force a child to eat. If food is not wanted take it away.
- Let her tell you when she is hungry.
- Try to have a casual manner where food is concerned. Take it or leave it, this is dinner.
- Do not let her eat snacks like crisps, sweets or milk, which will stave off hunger.
- When she asks for food later on, offer the refused meal again calmly.
- Rarely let your child eat something different from any one else in the family.
- Allow your little girl live with the consequences of her actions. In other words, if she refuses to eat the dinner you cooked, she goes hungry. Next time she does not refuse. If you cook an alternative or let her snack out, she knows she can manipulate you. Do this within reason if she really dislikes a particular vegetable but don't pressurise or make her finish, just calmly take away the plate.
- If she tends to be a difficult eater, offer her a choice then she will be more likely to eat the dinner once made. But again if she refuses, calmly remove it and cover it in the fridge. Then just say, 'Ok, you are not hungry, let me know when you are, your dinner is here ready for you.'

Other Difficulties

DISLIKES – if your child has certain dislikes, for example hates anything green, acknowledge the dislike without any sign of irritation or anxiety. Of course you may feel irritation because sometimes fads have no logic to them (I understand it's frustrating but try not to show it). Try serving a tiny portion of the disliked food on the side; one day she may try it and discover that her tastes have changed.

SUBTERFUGE – this may be required if she never eats fruits or vegetables. Use the list on how to 'tempt the fussy eater' and you could discover that the child who dislikes eggs may accept egg custard, pancakes or even decide that an egg whipped up with mashed potatoes can be very tasty.

WEIGHT – if you are worried that your child is losing or not gaining weight, or putting on too much weight, do discuss this with the public health nurse or GP.

A healthy diet should include...
- Fruit and vegetables.
- Carbohydrates, such as bread, pasta, potatoes and cereals.
- Protein, like meat, fish, pulses, eggs, cheese.
- Milk or milk-like foods, such as yoghurt.
- Water, which could be taken alone or in diluted fruit.

REMEMBER ... If you don't buy in junk food, sweets or fizzy drinks, your children can't eat them.

Other Tips to Try
- Make food look attractive with different brightly coloured vegetables like peas and sweet corn.
- Stick to regular meal times.
- Give smaller portions.
- Cut down on snacks between meals.
- Keep to the simple, plain foods.
- Let her choose the plate and cutlery herself. She may enjoy setting the table with fancy napkins and flowers – make it fun.
- If your child does not like meat, don't force it. Offer fish or cheese. If vegetables are unpopular, try to give more fruit.
- Changing the surroundings can work wonders. Have dinner in the garden or as a teddy bear's picnic or in the den or playhouse.
- Keep treats or desserts hidden until dinner is eaten; everyone should stay at the table until dinner is finished.

HOW SHOULD I PREPARE MY CHILD FOR SCHOOL?

Whether school was a positive or negative experience for us, we should do our best to make it as enjoyable an experience as possible for our children. It can be a daunting prospect for children who have not attended some type of playgroup previously. For those who went to any type of play school, the transition can be less traumatic. I have seen many a mother peeping through the window of the junior infants class to check her little darling is OK. I've also seen mothers crying more than their children because it can be just as big a step for Mummy losing her baby to school. Try not to let your child see you cry because it could upset her, although I do understand the mixture of emotions.

Is She Ready for School?

Putting a child into school when she is not emotionally ready does not give her a head start. In fact, it could be counterproductive. Being bright and being ready is not the same thing. Most children are ready at 5 years but if your child's birthday is around the cut off date, it may be difficult to know whether to hold the child back or let her go to school early.

Check Her Readiness for School

SPEECH – has she had any problems? If so being a little older may help her as they must be able to understand and be understood. Otherwise she will have a difficult time in the classroom.

HEALTH – any birth or health difficulties may have slowed up your child's development just a little. Again being a little older may enable them to cope better.

MATURIING – does she still have a nap in the daytime? Does she have a short attention span? If sitting still is not easy for her, wait a while.

DEVELOPMENT – has she fine motor skills, can she hold a pencil? Can she colour things in? Does she understand basics like shapes, sizes and colours?

INDEPENDENT – is she quite independent? Would she find the separation from you difficult? Would it be better to delay school until she is more confident?

SEX – boys tend to need more time before attending school than girls.

EXPERIENCE – does she have any pre-school experience? Children who do tend to fare better in big school, so the younger child could be fine in this case.

CHANGES – if there have been changes within the family, such as moving house, separation, divorce or a death, it may be unfair to give the child a new school to contend with as well.

DECISION – having taken all these into consideration and talked to the teachers at the school involved, make the decision about what time is best for your child to enter school life.

Getting Them Ready for School
- Play 'school' at home, getting other children involved and role-playing so that they will know what to expect.
- Let her attend a playgroup to get group experience.
- Buy or get a book from the library about starting school and read it together

45

- Talk about your own first day at school. For example, you had 'butterflies' of excitement in your tummy but you were a bit apprehensive, too. It was strange at first but you made new friends etc. Be realistic, warm and optimistic.

- Ensure she knows how to dress herself and go to the toilet alone. Choose clothing that is easy to pull on and off.

- Make sure she understands simple instructions and explain what her teacher may say and why.

- Put her name onto all her belongings, including clothes, bags, coat, cardigans and shoes. The best bag buys are the lightweight backpacks.

- Get her into the habit of getting her clothes ready the night before and dressing before breakfast.

- Purchase schoolbooks early to avoid the rush or they may get out of stock.

- Cover all the books; they'll last longer that way. The transparent sheeting is good.

- Visit the school and teacher before term begins. Visit the classroom. Teach her the layout, where the coats go, where the toilets are, so she will not feel lost.

- Whenever you pass the school say, 'Look, there is your school!' That way she'll get used to the route.

- Make sure she knows her name, telephone number and address. The name will be on books, coat hook or locker so she needs to know it.

- It is an advantage if she already knows her alphabet, how to count to 10 and has read with you regularly. Teach her.

- Set up a night and morning routine just before she starts school, so getting up will be natural when school starts.

- Give your child a special gift when she starts school, like a funny alarm clock, a special pencil case or a little beanie toy to pop in her bag.

- If she has a comfort toy that is special to her, let her take it to school until she settles in.

School Days

COLLECTION – make sure she knows whom and at what time someone will be back to collect her; try to let it be you on the first day.

SAFETY – make sure that she knows *never* to go with anyone other than the people you have told her about.

CRYING – if she cries and wants to leave or for you to stay remain a little longer. Then be firm, say, 'I am going' and go, letting the teacher know you are having difficulties so that she can take over. Peep in later to reassure yourself she is OK but do not let her see you. She has to learn to settle in without you. Crying is a natural emotion. It releases tension and can make us feel better – and that includes the parent!

PUNCTUALITY – please try to be on time when picking her up.

BE PREPARED – some children behave irritably or out of sorts when they first start school. This will pass. It is because of all the changes, which can be very tiring for our little ones. Or they may become shy, withdrawn, clingy or just bold. Don't worry; this should be just temporary.

LISTEN – after school ask what happened and listen carefully, so that you will be able to spot any troubled areas.

T.L.C. (Tender Loving Care) – give her a kiss, cuddle and one-to-one attention when she gets home. Lots of T.L.C. is important, even if she is behaving boldly, probably because she's exhausted. Be extra understanding.

DISCUSS – if she is having any problems settling in, go and discuss it with the teacher.

NEW FRIENDS – encourage any friendships by inviting others home after school to play.

UNDERSTANDING – share and talk about her new routine in the day so that you can understand her school life.

Other Suggestions

- Do remember the teachers' and friends' names and get involved in the school life as much as possible.
- Try having a timer that you can set for dressing or play time prior to school, or time to be ready to leave for school in the mornings.
- Stick to the same ideas for older child. Remember that the move from primary to secondary school often happens at the same time as changes occur both inside the body and emotionally. So plenty of T.L.C. and attention are needed at this transition time.

CHAPTER 2

5 to 12
– The Middle Years

IF I DON'T SMACK WHAT DO I DO?

Smacking: The Pros and Cons

When you have a newborn baby, you look down on her with loving eyes and may think you would never dream of smacking her. Yet most parents do at some stage. One research unit found that 62% of mothers smack their baby before she is 1 year old and that 68% smack their 4 year olds up to 6 times a week. It found that smacking is common in all social backgrounds and that it decreases as the child gets older. Another found that 90% of children are physically punished. Here are some arguments for and against.

Reasons Given For Smacking

1. That a totally non-smacking policy is unrealistic. You need first rate parenting skills, ideal home conditions and a degree in child psychology for it to work.

2. A smack does no harm as a deterrent for persistent bold behaviour.

3. Used as a last resort for repeated bad behaviour.

4. Used especially where safety is involved. For example, on a screaming, kicking child who refuses to get into her car seat.

5. I was smacked and it did me no harm.

6. If there is no smacking then the children have nothing to fear and think they can do anything.

Reasons Given For Not Smacking

1. It is wrong to hit adults, so it is wrong to hit children.

The child is usually shocked that a beloved parent would hurt them and is often terrified and humiliated.

2.   Even good motives do not make it right to hit anyone, especially vulnerable children.

3.   Where do you draw the line between what is a smack and what is child abuse?

4.   It is not an effective form of punishment or teaching. Smacking teaches children it is OK to use physical force to solve problems.

5.   Usually done in anger as a release, it does not work and makes you feel like a bully afterwards.

6.   Parents who abuse their children often say it started off with an 'ordinary' smack.

Of course there are many more reasons why different parents feel they should or should not smack. Here's one good reason – it simply does not work as well as good parenting discipline. That is one of the reasons that I wrote this book, because many of the parents I worked with did not want to smack but did not know how else to deal with difficult situations that arose and resorted to smacking.

Alternatives to Smacking

SETTING LIMITS – and being firm. Set reasonable limits that are firm and predictable, so she knows what will happen if she disobeys.

CONSISTENCY – meaning what you say, so that *No* today is *No* tomorrow. Be consistent and think carefully before you say *No*, because you'll need to say it every time.

LIMITED CHOICE – for example, 'You can stop fighting or go to your room' or 'You can put your shoes on and play outside or you can play inside and leave your shoes off.'

CONSEQUENCES – by allowing children to live with the consequences of their actions, you can let them see what happens. For example, if they're fighting over T.V. programmes, say, 'You can work out a solution yourselves, taking turns at watching the programmes, or I can turn the TV off. The choice is yours.' If the fighting continues, the TV goes off, no messing, and stays off. The next night there will be no fights.

AVOID BATTLES – you cannot win, whether it's picking up toys or making her eat her dinner. Is it really worth it? Keep the rules and things that you insist on to a minimum.

EXPLAIN – *why* rules matter, using words that she can understand. For example, 'Throwing toys may hurt someone, and break the toy.'

PUNISHMENT – if you need to punish, explain the reason why, such as she could hurt herself or someone else. Warn her what the punishment is, and if the misbehaviour continues, carry it out! Empty threats do not work. No favourite cartoon today or no visiting your friend's house – and keep to it! Children feel safer if you are firm rather than indulgent.

PRAISE – do not forget to also reward and praise good behaviour.

ARGUMENTS – talk one-to-one with your child everyday. This gives you an opportunity to sort out any arguments that you may have had during the day.

FEELINGS – encourage your child to talk about uncomfortable feelings like envy, anger or jealousy. They are much better out than in. Accept these feelings and talk about them.

WALK AWAY – don't be afraid to just walk away and do some deep breathing or count to ten if you feel like smacking your child. That realistically happens to most parents at some stage.

GUILT – if you do ever smack your child (and this can happen to any parent with every intention of not smacking), leave the room to have a chance to calm down and then come back to apologise and explain why it happened. Try not to feel guilty – it is such an unproductive emotion and it could happen to a bishop/me/anyone. Your child will respect you for being truthful.

MY YOUNGSTERS ARE CONSTANTLY SQUABBLING – WHAT'S A PARENT TO DO?

Q

Strategies For Coping With Arguments

Why does it sometimes seem that children are fighting all the time? There is nothing that makes a parent despair like constant squabbling. But be consoled that arguments do happen at times in nearly every family household in the world. That acknowledged, how can we try to get a more peaceful household? Firstly, let's try to get to the bottom of why they fight.

Ask Yourself...
* Is there an underlying problem?
* What happened before and after the row?

- Is there a reason the child behaved like that? Is she tired? Frustrated? Over excited?
- What happened just prior to the row? Was there a warning? A trigger?
- What was your child trying to achieve by this? Is it just attention seeking? Is angry attention better than no attention?

Remember emotions run high with children. They feel passionately about nearly everything. They have to learn to control themselves. This is all part of emotional development. At times they may seem to turn into monsters, whereas most of the time they are little angels... well, children anyway!

Sometimes there may be no real reason for the fight. The more people there are in a family, the more the children have to learn to compromise and share, whether it's material things or their parents' love. There is also a positive side to rows. Although such rows may upset you greatly and you may be alarmed by the aggression shown towards each other, remember that it is generally 'safe' to row at home and it prepares them for the outside world. They learn about diplomacy, compromise and how things can get out of hand, but at home you are there to guide them.

How To Stop The Rows

1.   Make a list of the rules you expect to be followed. Spend some time working it out. Make sure you have realistic expectations. What do you really expect her to do and not to do? For examples, not hitting her younger brother/ tidying her room once a week/coming straight home from school.

2.   Go over the list to check if it is reasonable. What purpose does it serve? Ask yourself does it protect her and the family; teach important values, like honesty; spread the

family chores; give equality; stop physical violence? Have a short precise list of the basic important rules.

3. Now it is time for a Family Meeting. Pick a calm relaxed time, then say how you feel, perhaps something like, 'I'm unhappy about the constant rowing.' Have a discussion, allowing everyone to have time to speak and give suggestions, then bring out the list and ask for their comments. Is it fair to ask this? To work effectively, everyone needs to agree that a few changes may need to be made. If they feel some are unfair, explain why they are necessary, giving reasons. Be firm but open for discussion. Once decided on, put the list up in a central place to act as a reminder; everyone could sign the bottom of the list, 'The family rules to encourage a happy home.'

4. The next step is to talk about rewards and punishments. Discuss what rewards there are for reaching the goals set down and what punishments will be handed out if the rules are broken. Let the children have a major role in choosing the rewards and punishment, within reason. This could cause a lively fun discussion. Any suggestions that a suitable punishment could be an hour's extra play on the computer would, of course, be treated as a great joke. Nice try, next idea!

Alternatives

Younger children may respond better to a star chart, winning stars or smiling faces for each rule followed, with 5-7 stars = reward. The reward can be an extra treat, an additional 15 minutes before going bed, or whatever would please your child and you. But please make the rewards worthwhile for the children – given that, the arguments will hopefully occur less often.

There are bound to be the odd flash points. Here is what to do:–

Avoiding Rows

- Try to find out what is the major cause of the rowing. Then discuss with the children a way in which it could be stopped.
- Fighting can break out if children are cooped up in a confined space. Get them outside to space and fresh air if you can. Then they can run off that excess energy.
- Some children hate to share rooms. If they have to, make sure they have well-defined areas, which are their own space.
- Try to anticipate when a row may occur and avoid it by taking certain measures beforehand. For example, mornings can be busy and rushed so avoid a confrontation by having everything organised the night before... bags ready, packed lunches done.
- Avoid confrontations, especially at stressful times. Distract or make a joke.
- Don't rise to the bait. Whinging, complaining, showing off, or rudeness can be reduced by simply ignoring it.
- Give a good example by trying to control your temper, and do not row.

What To Do If Squabbling Occurs

Firstly, try to avoid getting involved in the children's squabbles unless absolutely necessary. Refuse to give attention to their bold behaviour. Instead give attention later, when they are behaving nicely, when they least expect it. Leave the room and let them get on with it.

If there is a danger of someone being hurt and you feel you have to intervene, do so calmly, avoiding making snap decisions or judgements about who may be to blame, as this will seem very unjust to the children involved.

Calmly separate them and say something to try and identify with the child's emotions like, 'You both sound very upset and angry, what is happening here?' They both may try to speak at once. Allow them both the time to speak and explain their position, hopefully with each listening to the other's point of view, but then taking them aside or to another room, if necessary.

Repeat back to them what they have told you. For example saying, 'Now let me get this straight, you tripped her and she punched you,' etc. You might ask thought-provoking questions like, 'How do you feel about that?' or 'How would you feel if she'd done that to you?' Once calm again, put them together and ask them if they feel there is any solution to the problem – they are both basically kind, clever kids so you feel you could leave them to sort it out, and leave the room, with a warning that you will separate them permanently if fighting commences again.

If necessary, help them to compromise by giving them alternatives to which they can relate without having to back down and lose face.

Stay calm. I really know how hard this can be, but it is so important that you are in control ... take a run around the block to relieve your frustration afterwards, if you must! And *never* take sides.

Children usually develop better self-control when they're around 7 years old. If they do not, look for an underlying cause and the example you are setting.

If punishments are necessary, explain to the children in words they can understand why you are doing it. For example, 'You cannot have a temper tantrum like that and shout at everyone. This family has a right to a peaceful and happy home so go to your room and think about that until you can come back and treat us in a more kindly manner.'

If anger is shown and goes unchecked by a parent, a child may use it to manipulate the family to get her own way. So talk about expressing anger in others ways perhaps with exercise or creatively.

Positive Tips
- Don't expect too much, too quickly – the rowing will not

just stop because you've made a list and are trying. It takes time!

- *Be consistent* – this is the key to success.
- Always praise when they try, and reward when they do behave well. Keep to the positive; do not just keep doling out the punishments.
- When you talk to your children, get down to their level. Do not talk down to them but firmly and clearly make sure they understand you and know that you mean business.
- Try to remember the times they do get on well and play happily together. They will be friends again soon, honestly!

MY DAUGHTER SEEMS TO WHINGE ALL THE TIME – HOW CAN I HANDLE THIS?

HANDLING ATTENTION SEEKING

Ways to stop the whinging!

It is a rainy day with a dull, grey sky outside. The baby is crying, your little darling woke up in a bad mood and has had a tantrum already this morning and is whinging again already. How can we cope with this and stay sane? Let's take this *step-by-step*.

There is always a reason for this whinging so look for it! Why is she behaving like this? Is she still tired, did she not get a good night's sleep, could she benefit from another little nap? If she does not like the idea of going back to bed and tears ensue, make a cuddly bed on the couch with her favourite toy and blanket, tell her a story or turn on a story tape. Let her rest or have a nap. If you feel like it, pop her in the buggy – you'll get your exercise and she'll get a nap, or the fresh air may brighten her up.

Check her temperature, is she sickly? If so, contact your GP. If teething, try chamomile granules to soothe her.

If you cannot find any particular reason why she may be whinging, it may be that she is miserable and just attention seeking. The problem is that if you give attention when she is behaving boldly, you are rewarding the attention-seeking behaviour i.e. I whinge – I get Mum's attention. If she gets attention, it works and then she'll do it again, and a cycle of whinging has started.

Ask yourself, 'Am I giving her enough attention in the right way and at the right time?' Be honest, are you giving her one-to-one attention regularly? If not, try to make amends.

There is no magic solution, you cannot just wave a wand and expect her behaviour to change instantly. However, we can start to give attention at the correct time and turn the mood around.

Attention Seeking Behaviour

The attention-seeking child is not usually a happy one; she may feel discouraged or even bad about herself, and she does not upset you on purpose. The child just keeps you busy whinging, refusing to eat or just by being plain difficult, when really she only wants loving attention.

What To Do

Do not reward the whinging by giving it any attention. Any attention, even nagging, complaining or scolding the child, is giving it attention albeit negative attention. The child will take any attention she can get. Practise ignoring it and try to switch off. Then when she is behaving normally and nicely, start to give her positive attention. This is difficult to do when you have a busy household to run.

Here are a few fun ideas to chase away the blues that you may both enjoy:–

- If it's a horrible rainy day, kit her out with wellies and a Mac with a hood and let her go puddle jumping. Watch her jump around enjoying herself, praise and have fun with here. No more grumps.
- If you are busy, let her help you. As you tidy around, put her on a chair at the sink, with an apron on her, with a bowl full with lots of warm water and bubbles, and let her wash the non-breakables. She'll do it for ages.
- Fill a big box with goodies, old hats, skirts blouses, jewellery, shoes, handbags, things she does not usually play with and let her have fun.
- If she's getting on your nerves, get out of the house it doesn't matter where. Change the scene. Go to the shops, let her pick and carry things. Go to the library, let her choose her own books, or to the park and let her have a good run around, and go on a nature trail together.
- Create a secret den for her made out of blankets, or sheets draped over a line, a chair or the sofa. She can furnish then with dolls, books, a torch etc.
- Put music on and let her have a dance. Give her a few spoons and saucepans to play along with the music.
- Have a five-minute exercise session together.
- Under stress? Have a picnic lunch in the den made out of bite-sized little sandwiches, cubes of cheese and slices of fruit – make it easy on yourself.
- Or have a shower of bath together and relax with each other.

Other Tactics

You feel you have given her lots of loving attention and she is still whinging. So what next?

1. Ignore her.

2. Try leaving her alone for a few minutes and she may just calm down and do something for herself.

3.   Are you being realistic or trying to do too much? Life is short – slow the pace down. If you're stressed out she may be reacting to you. If you are not dealing well with your own anger and stresses, a child can easily pick this up.

4.   Leave the house chores until later on. Do only the essentials and sit back and relax with your daughter.

5.   Avoid nagging or losing your temper. It only makes matters worse and she'll whinge more.

6.   Get on to her level – talk calmly and firmly, saying, 'Enough crying'. Give her a big, loving cuddle, tell what you are going to do now and do it. Leave a book, toy or jigsaw or something to play with nearby, and hopefully that will distract her and give her something to do.

7.   Ask her what is making her so unhappy.

8.   Attention seeking and misbehaviour generally needs an audience – stay silent and/or leave the room, and see what happens. They say a change is as good as a rest. Sometimes a change of approach works, too.

MY CHILD HITS OTHER CHILDREN AND SOMETIMES ME. WHY DOES HE HAVE TO GET INTO FIGHTS?

Coping With Unacceptable Behaviour

There are many reasons why a child hits another child or adult. These include:–

SHARING – Very young children have not learned how to share, so they just lash out. They feel that the toy or whatever they have is almost part of them. They do it to get what they want, so you need to teach them other reasonable ways of getting what they want or explain that we all can't have what we want, giving an example.

UNHAPPY – If a child is unhappy, 'out of sorts' or just irritable, she may just hit out to take it out on the person nearest to her, whether it's you, a friend, a sister, a brother.

BOSS – A child may hit out to show she cannot be pushed or bossed about.

EMOTION – When a child can't find the right things to say, the emotional overflows into the physical. Teach her to use brains not brawn.

ATTENTION – Another big reason is our old friend, attention seeking. The child reckons that the person she hits is bound to take notice and go crazy.

I do not like children hitting and/or fighting, but there is always a certain amount of rowing within the family, which often spills over into physical fighting. It is unacceptable behaviour but normal, when there is sibling rivalry in a family. While a certain amount of fighting within the family is normal, it is how we cope with it as a parent that is very important.

How to Prevent and Deal with Hitting and Fighting

Have *no violence* as a basic family, so they know it is totally unacceptable behaviour. Let them know this as a certainty. Also give them a good example; if you hit they will think that they can.

With a young child, say 'No' firmly and remove her from the scene and leave her in isolation for a while to think about what she has done. Then consider why she did it and ask her why. If she wanted a toy, talk about an alternative way to get the toy. Explain why hitting is not allowed and the hurt it causes. Ask her to apologise. You could warn her that she will be punished if it happens again, and how. Do not be dramatic, just calm and firm.

In the Family Context

- Do ignore play fighting as much as you can.
- Don't rise to the bait. Allow them to have a little tussle; sometimes they even enjoy the fight.
- Try to make every child feel that little bit special, keeping jealousy down to a minimum.
- Do what you can to keep children active and busy, and give outlets for any frustration that may arise.
- Teach them to ignore teasing and other tactics; children may try to goad each other into a fight.
- If an argument is getting out of hand, suggest 'time out' to go their separate ways, before blows are struck.
- Hungry children are more likely to fight. If they have to wait for dinnertime, let them have a wholesome snack when they arrive home from school.
- Have a timer and set it, telling them that the argument must end when it goes off.
- If the children are starting to row, say something jokey to defuse their anger.
- A child with food sensitivities can be irritable, as can a sickly child. See your GP for advice. Avoid allergens.
- If a child is physically hitting another, hold her firmly and securely from behind and lead her away, and isolate.
- Do not forget to praise when they are playing happily and not misbehaving. Be sure to communicate with your children fully and freely when all goes well in the household, so that they do not need to misbehave to gain your attention.

Finally, a word about punishments. As parents, you are in the best position to know what punishments suit your child and its temperament. 'Time Out' can be enough, as can the taking away of privileges, or making them do extra chores. Follow through with what you warn, but try to keep any punishments to a minimum, praising good behaviour and being positive rather than negative!

WHY DOES MY SON ALWAYS ANSWER ME BACK?

How To Use Words Effectively

I understand what this question is saying, but the way it is worded seems to me that this parent and child have a communication problem. A conversation needs two people in it. So it must be the tone and disrespect in the answer the parent does not like. However, I feel a slightly superior tone in the question and I just wonder if the child feels this, too. So here are some important points to remember when we are talking to our children. Follow them and your communication with your children will improve.

When Talking With Children...

- Do not talk down to children.
- Learn to listen well. A child may find it hard to come straight out with a problem. Do not be too quick to find a solution. She may find her own.
- Encourage talking by saying things like, 'How did that make you feel?' or 'What did you hope for?'
- If a child talks in an angry way, remember it is not necessarily directed at you. It will help to get the feelings off her chest.
- If a child wants to talk and you have not got the time then apologise and say, 'I am busy now but I would love to talk about it later' and do.

- Always talk, talk, listen, listen, listen, and communicate; it gets more difficult with teenagers but keep trying.
- Do not be judgmental when talking; keep an open mind. Don't attack with questions.
- Respect your child's privacy. Don't pressurise her into talking but let her know you are there if she needs to talk and you can be trusted to have her best interests at heart.
- Actions can also be a language. Door slamming, foot stamping and big sighs are ways of expressing how we feel. Instead of saying, 'Stop that' try saying, 'I can see you are in an angry mood - would you like to talk about it?'
- Do not tell your child off in front of friends or family. If you have something to say take her aside or in another room to say it.
- Learn to be a good *listener*, maintaining eye-to-eye contact. Do not look around or do other things when she is talking to you. *Actively* listen, let her know you are interested.
- Do not deny your child's feelings. If she says, 'I hate maths' do not say, 'No you don't'. Instead say something like, 'You sound very negative about Maths today. Are you finding it very difficult?'
- Avoid lecturing.
- Remember that it is sometimes not *what we say* but *how we say it*. *Attitude* is very important. It can put a totally different message across, depending on the way we say things.
- Do not shout because they will just switch off. If you want them to listen to you, go close and say it right to them at their level.
- Try not to moralise.
- Be brief in your comments. As a child of mine remarked, 'Adults are so long-winded.'
- When talking, grant your child the genuine respect due to a human being.

Remember, if you speak to your children respectfully they will most probably return the compliment. If they don't, explain that it is not nice to be spoken to in that manner. And remember that it is important to have the right environment for a talk. Just prior to bed is a nice time for a cosy chat. A long walk is a good time for a long discussion on an important issue. Always give them time to say their piece. Finally, listen to yourself when you talk to your children ... you may be surprised at what you hear.

WHAT SHOULD I DO ABOUT MY CHILDREN'S CONTINUOUS TEASING OF EACH OTHER?

Sibling Rivalry

There is always some sort of *conflict* in a family. People can get hassled and things can get 'out of hand'. Negative interaction can occur between sister and brother or sister and sister or brother and brother, in the form of shouting matches, hair pulling, biting, scratching and teasing. Also emotional efforts can be made to 'get what you want' - you can always call on mother for help, pout, sulk or pester, blackmail, threaten to tell, bribe or even flatter. If none of these things happen in your home, then count yourself lucky.

What To Do?

Discuss as parents what are the best ways to handle these disputes and then both follow the same steps. Together work out step by step how both of you will react if an argument starts. That way you both react in the same way and there is consistency. As we have discussed in the question on constant squabbling, both of you may decide that you are going to simply ignore these inter-family disputes until you must go in to save someone being hurt.

Alternatively you may choose to 'nip them in the bud', choosing to step in and separate them as soon as a conflict looks as if it is becoming unruly. Or you may simply give a 'time out,' warning them that they know from past experiences that the next step is separation and isolation.

Children fight for many reasons. It could be a *power struggle* but power is only important if it is fought for. However, if they are unable to draw you in they'll have lost at the start so *don't be drawn in.* If TV or radio is on, turn them off or voice levels will rise and shouting will ensue.

Attention seeking is a very common reason for fighting. It is a way of saying, 'Pay attention to me.' I win only if am successful so *ignore* as much as you can and if you need to get involved, *isolate* so they still don't get the attention they want. Instead, give them attention when their behaviour is good and co-operative.

Give them a quiet cooling off period to think about what happened. Stay calm when things have settled down, later have a gentle talk about what happened. Chances are if you stayed calm and did not over-react to the action that they'll already feel bad or sorry.

Positive Ways To Discourage Sibling Rivalry

LOVE – A child must feel loved to be happy. If she knows she is loved and feels secure, she is more likely to share and respect others more readily. Cherish your child and let her know by actions and words that you do.

EXAMPLE – From an early age, show by example. Let her see how to care by sharing things with family, friends and neighbours. She'll learn to give and take by being shared with. Help her to understand the value of sharing, then your child will grow up believing this is the right way to behave and will respond by being generous.

EMOTIONS – A child needs to be able to express how she feels and how to deal with emotions, both negative and positive. Give her enough time and attention in the good times. By giving her time to talk as you listen, you will show you care.

POINTS OF VIEW – Children need to be helped sometimes to see the other point of view and to realise that other people have the same feelings, desires and upsets. Once they start to understand and sympathise with others they will be less likely to upset them by causing fights.

LEARN – Even when you do all this, your children will not be happy and well behaved *all* the time. That's life, like a box of chocolates with different centres.

Questions To Ask Yourself...

- Is there a pattern to the fights? Consider making notes and note if there are special times, patterns or triggers to be found.

- Are these battles masking another underlying problem? Could school or parents really be the problem? It is easier to hit a little sister than a Dad.

- Are you taking their fighting personally? Think of it as a growth and teasing time. Remind yourself that all children row sometimes and that home is a safe place to practise conflict-resolution skills.

- Are you projecting wars on your children by choosing favourites, therefore causing competition?

- Are you insisting too much that they should be friends? All children are different and unique – accept them as such.

MY CHILD IS SO DIFFICULT. DO YOU HAVE ANY TIPS ON HANDLING HER?

Q

Consider the headstrong, strong-willed, difficult and just plain bold or, if a parent is trying to be positive, 'spirited' child. Have you got one of those children? Does your child have tantrums regularly? Is she sensitive to any changes in her routine? Does she hate to be confined to a room, to the house, to be buckled safely in the car? Can she not sit still for long?

The list can go on. Does she insist on picking her clothes and dressing herself, no matter how inappropriately? Does she make a mess wherever she goes? Is she a picky or fussy eater? Do you feel that she is manipulating you sometimes?

Remember though that the child who causes a lot of breakages, makes a mess or keeps touching things, is just a curious little creature. These things are not naughty but rather signs of an inquisitive child with high spirits. So although I know children like this can be exhausting, try to keep it in the right perspective.

Children who have fiery temperaments can be handled in a certain way, so that at least a parent can work with the temperament rather than against it. For if a parent works against the grain of prickly temperaments, it can lead to constant confrontations and a very upset household.

Parents who have one of these energetic, mischievous children may blame themselves for the child's conduct. Perhaps they feel they did not give enough limits to the child, or the discipline boundaries were too wide or were moved too often when they were younger.

While there may be reasons for a child misbehaving, it must also be taken into account that 'wilfulness' may be part of a child's nature. It is also worth noting that children are not aware they are manipulating you – there is no malice intended. They do not (when they are very young) set out to manipulate Mummy. That, of course, may come later if this stage is not handled in a calm but firm way.

However, if they behave in a certain way, such as throwing a tantrum because they do not want to go to bed and are then allowed to stay up, they will learn that the behaviour worked because their needs were satisfied. Therefore they will repeat the successful (in their mind) behaviour. Unfortunately that means that a parent will have to put up with more tantrums rather than less. As parents, we must always have an eye to *the consequences of our actions*.

Genetics do have a part to play. If you talk to grand-parents, they will really enjoy telling a spouse that, 'Johnny was just the same. He drove me crazy at times, never sat still for a minute.'

Many times a child like this will rush around excitedly then get exhausted and be emotionally up and down throughout the day. So what are we parents to do with this bundle of energy?

Channelling Your Child's Emotions and Energy

STAY CALM – Do not allow your child's emotional ups and down get to you. Do not swing with her but stay calm and consistent as possible. This will help even out her own moods and give her a good example to follow. (I know this is easier said then done, but do your best).

WARNINGS – When any changes are about to occur, like leaving a friend's house, going to bed, having dinner, *give plenty of warnings*.

INSTRUCTIONS – When you need her to do something turn off any distractions like TV, radio or games. Get down to her eye level. Be clear and precise in your instructions, make sure she listens and knows you mean business. Be direct!

TANTRUMS – If she has a tantrum, tell yourself that she is just overwhelmed with emotions and looking for help, not just being bold (it helps you cope). Have a set plan to follow if a tantrum occurs and stick to it. It will comfort both of you. This plan depends on your personal choice. It could be to firmly cuddle the child, whispering all will be well, or it could be to leave the room and let the tantrum with no audience subside in its own time (see Tantrums p. 28).

CONFLICT – If you start the day with a heated battle about clothes, this may continue all day. A strong-willed child would be better having plenty of time in the mornings, rather than being rushed. So get up a little earlier and let her pick the clothes to wear the night before. Avoiding conflict about lunches, food, clothes or whatever before playschool or school helps the day to run smoother.

BEHAVIOUR – Pay extra attention when your child helps or behaves well. Try to ignore any annoying behaviour or fiddling, whining or rushing about, until you have to intervene.

ACTIVITIES – Because they are very active children, give them lots of physical activities to do so that they can burn off their excess energy. Join any local groups, playgroups, beavers, scouts, anchor-girls or boys, brownies, sports clubs, dancing classes, so that they can channel their energies in fun ways.

HELPING – Do not underestimate how this child can help you. Dusting, gardening, setting the table, hanging out the clothes – let them know how much you appreciate it when they do. 'Well done, Love, what a good job, thanks you're a great help to me.'

TAKE A BREAK – Finally give yourself a well-earned break

regularly. These children can be great fun, but can be exceptionally tiring and emotionally draining. If you have little breaks from this type of child it will help you keep your composure and counterbalance your child's emotional shifts. Talk with partners, families and friends, let them know you will need time to yourself on a regular basis, and keep your sense of proportion and humour – these children can be great jokers.

MY CHILDREN DO NOT COME WHEN I CALL. HOW CAN I MAKE THEM ATTEND TO ME?

Teaching Children to Co-Operate and how to Live with the Consequences of their Actions

We are back to the question of how can we get our children to do as we ask, without using force. Here is an example:

> Your child will not get up in the morning when you call. Time after time you are up and down the stairs, urging and coaxing, but nothing works and you all end up bad tempered. It upsets the household. What do you do?

You discuss the problem with her, listening carefully and putting your point of view forward. Make sure there are no distractions and you both listen to each other's point of view and come to an arrangement.

If this does not work the next step could be to give her an alarm clock of her own and teach her how to set it. You decide with her and the family what is a good time to rise so everyone has enough time for washing and breakfast. Then say the exact time you intend to leave in the car or she has to get the bus. State that from now on that is the time you are going to leave and stick by it! Anyone not ready at that time must deal with the consequences of getting to school late, facing detention or getting in trouble with the teacher.

Allow for genuine reasons for being late but otherwise *be firm* and stick with your side of the agreement. If you give in and take her after she has stayed in bed or caused trouble again, she'll know that she can manipulate you. If, however, you stand firm, she will know she will have to co-operate or get into great difficulties.

This way, she is also learning to look after herself. You are allowing her to choose to co-operate or suffer the real *consequences* of her behaviour. This is the same throughout life – the logical conclusion to a person's actions is a lesson we all must learn. Remember this as you explain, saying 'No, you got up late and have to live with the consequences. We agreed and you broke the agreement. Go to school now and let's try it again tomorrow, and with a bit of luck things will go better.' Keep your voice calm not agitated, be firm but gentle. You are not doing this as a punishment but as a learning process. She may shout or get upset, but you should stay calmly firm.

Discipline is essential, but that does not mean forcing or necessarily punishing. It means having rules and ensuring that they are carried out, *letting the children live with the consequences of their actions*. Thus you must have the strength to *stay firm*, even when you feel sorry for her getting to school late.

During regular family meetings involve your children in the running of the family home. Discuss things like bed times at weekends and school days, chores all the children can do, times for schools or outings, or any problems they or you may be having, as well as ways that they could help you and each other. It teaches them responsibility. Do not discuss any difficult issue when tensions are already high.

Speak in a calm, positive way and be careful how you say everything. Being domineering, saying something like, 'You'll do as you are told' would make anyone feel like rebelling. Instead, try 'Yes, you can watch the TV once you have tidied your room,' speaking in a positive, non-judgmental way and giving her the choice. Let her make the right decision without losing face. Afterwards say, 'Good, your room looks great now. It's a great help when you all keep your room in order. You can see where everything is.'

Children who get their own way all the time are spoilt and are protected from their own actions by 'well meaning' parents. They are usually unhappy children. All children need limits and rules – they feel secure and safe knowing the boundaries. Children who are taught to live with the consequences are eventually more responsible and it fosters good self-discipline for the future.

Finally this learning to live with the consequences of their own actions can be applied to many difficulties... the list is endless. For example, the child who refuses to eat goes hungry as a consequence; she will eat next time. If the warning of not being able to go to the movies unless chores are done is ignored, the consequence is no movie; next time she'll do her chores. Be firm.

Now consider ways that you could apply this rule of actions/consequences to other situations in your home.

MY DAUGHTER SEEMS TO BE SHY AND WITHDRAWN AROUND CHILDREN OF HER OWN AGE

Encouraging Self Worth

Children value themselves as they are valued. We all want to be accepted. We all want our children to grow up to be sociable, to have good friends and to be liked. It is seldom that any parent does not worry at least once about his/her child and her social standing. It is not just about being popular. It is about both having and being able to be a true friend. If a child knows how to share and co-operate, and has a sense of humour, she'll make friends easily. But we all have to work to keep friendships going.

By the time a child is 8 to 10 years old, she starts to realise that friendship is more then just giving and getting. But do not panic when you daughter comes in and says, 'No one in school likes me' or 'No one wants to play with me'. Or your teenager says, 'I am so ugly, I hate myself.' Self-doubt and being apprehensive about our abilities and friendships is all a part of growing up.

Here are some ways that a parent can help children develop social skills and develop self-esteem...

MANNERS – Teach your child to be polite from an early age. Saying, 'please' and 'thank you' and 'excuse me' shows the people around us that we are respectful of their feelings – a good step towards friendship.

SELF CONTROL – You help a young child to be friendly by teaching self-control. A child who has tantrums regularly, gets angry easily or is unpredictable is less likely to appear friendly than one who is thought to be even-tempered.

EXAMPLE – Be a good role model. Care for, respect and treasure your friends.

ACCEPTANCE – Accept your children the way they are. Some children will always be less outgoing than others.

SUPPORT – If your child has any areas of skill or appearance where she needs help or feels inadequate, support her. For example, if her reading is poor, encourage and read with her.

LISTEN – Listen to her and offer constructive advice if necessary, but don't just brush away as silly anything she has to say. If she feels that way, acknowledge her hurt.

CRISIS – Do not over-react if a friendship crisis has occurred. They tend to be short-lived. However, don't dismiss it lightly. Children can be very cruel to each other and to be left out is a terrible wound. Acknowledge the pain and sympathise. Perhaps tell a story about when you where hurt or left out in your youth.

TALENTS – If she cannot play sports, this will not always be so and there is always something everyone can do that they are good at – find it!

REJECTION – Ask her can she see any reason why she feels left out or whether she has any suggestions for changing the situation. Does she think that she has encouraged this seclusion in any way? It is sad, but dressing differently or behaving in certain ways can make a world of difference to children and friendships. Unfortunately being different, whether it's being over-weight, a different colour, or too good or too bad at something, can start off a pattern of rejection in a child's life

NUMBERS – Don't worry about the amount of friends a child has, or if she does not have a best friend. Just be sure she relates well to playmates and classmates.

AFFIRMATION – Give your child lots of *affirmation* and *affection*. The undervalued child feels insecure and in greater need of acceptance. Love your child, let her know it in words and actions.

TEACHERS – Talk with her *teacher*. Is she really being left out? If so, can the teacher help in any way? A good teacher, I have found, tries to teach much more than academic skills. They can help to teach social skills as well.

ACTIVITIES – Involve her in different activities where she

meets different people of all types. Perhaps a sports club, a girls' guide group, a book club, an orienteering group. What sort of thing does she like that will encourage mixing with others? If she finds something she is good at, this will develop her confidence and will carry over to all aspects of her life.

INTERACTION – Invite some of her friends over and observe how they interact. Can you see any pattern? Is she bossy? Unwilling to share? Are the friends OK?

NEGATIVE TRAITS – Do point out gently any negative traits you may find about her or her playmates in a tactful way. For example, 'I think the way Susan shouts at people is not a nice way to behave, do you?'

VALUES – If you speak about loyalty, generosity and friendship the message will sink in gradually. Ask her what values she likes in her friends.

You may find that it is not your daughter who has a problem but it is the friends she is associating with that are the problem. If so, you could...

1. Limit the contact, if you can. If not, make sure she has plenty of access to others who could be friends and nurture any other friendships.
2. Talk to the other parents.
3. Again, seek guidance from teachers, coaches or supervisory adults involved.
4. Ask yourself why your daughter likes this or these particular friends? Is there any way you could work on this?

• Encourage your child to invite her friends regularly after school or at weekends.

- Make your home a likeable pleasant place to hang out for children. Offer a friendly welcome and something nice to eat. You'll be able to see how she interacts, too … but
- don't hang around too long or let them notice.

If your child says she does not like the way she looks, don't say immediately, 'You're lovely, don't be silly.' Instead, listen. What is she really trying to say? Perhaps she just wants to talk for a while. Perhaps she's just saying, 'I feel lousy today'. Instead say, 'I think you look OK but what are you unhappy about?' You might suggest things like a new hair cut, for example, or even treatment for spots. But you may find that what is on her mind has nothing to do with the way she looks but something else entirely.

Get her to help others. Involving herself in doing things for others may help her to make friends / feel useful / feel needed and boost her self-confidence. Many voluntary organ-isations are crying out for helpers.

Respect and empathise with her feelings. Put yourself in her shoes and try to remember how you would have felt when you were a child and it happened to you. Things we think are silly now seemed very important then.

Realise you cannot make the world perfect for your child. It is painful for a parent to admit but our children will not be happy all the time. Just be there to guide, support and encourage in the bad times and tell them you love them whatever.

Especially For Teens

- Respect their need for privacy sometimes.
- Encourage independence. Help them to make their own decisions.
- Encourage them to bring their friends home.
- Do spend time with them regularly.

- *Listen* carefully. Find out what it is like to be a teenager in today's world.
- They love a joke. Keep a sense of humour and keep it light.

MY CHILD HATES SCHOOL. DO YOU THINK SHE COULD BE BEING BULLIED?

Q

There are times when children may come home and say, 'I hate school'. This is a time when you must sit down with a child and *listen* carefully to what may be going on. They say two in every five children are bullied at school at some stage.

So what do you do?

TALK/LISTEN – Set aside a time to talk but most importantly *listen* to what is going on at school.

FEELINGS – Encourage the child to talk about her feelings, such as jealousy, anger, envy, uselessness. Accept how she feels and be sympathetic – do not just brush them aside.

UNUSUAL BEHAVIOUR – Watch out if your child starts any new or unusual behaviour. She may indeed be trying to tell you something is wrong at school.

OTHER PROBLEMS – It may not be bullying it could be having difficulty with a new maths problem, not coping well with a certain subject, a personality conflict with a certain teacher or any number of things. *Listen* and find out what it is.

Signs of Bullying
A child may indicate there is a problem by displaying any of these possible signs:–

- Suddenly reluctant or unwilling to go to school.
- Being frightened to walk to or from school. Or changing their school route.
- Difficulty going to sleep or having nightmares.
- Losing appetite or coming home starving because her dinner has been stolen.
- Becoming more clingy. Confidence generally failing.
- Crying frequently or more easily, being distressed or becoming withdrawn, even starting to stammer.
- Has unexplained bruises or scratches.
- Have her possessions gone missing?
- Refuses to say what is wrong!

What To Do?

There are a number of things you can do if your child displays any of the above signs or just tells you she is being bullied.

- Take the bullying seriously and take positive action.
- Talk to the play leader or schoolteacher in charge of the group of children where the bullying has occurred.
- Offer your child *support* and *reassurance*. Give your child a chance to vent her feelings about what has happened. She should not feel she needs to cope alone.
- Try to discover if your child is the only one being bullied and enlist the help of any other parents involved.
- Help her with *practical strategies* to deal with any bullies like shouting, 'NO!' before walking away with confidence and head held high. Encourage her to laugh at them or ignore their comments.
- *Role play* certain situations and see how she reacts and think of ways in which she could react which would help deal with the situation. For example, if another child trips her, or demands money from her. Work it through – what do the bullies usually do and what should her reaction be? Teach her not to be drawn in case of danger.

- Teach her to stay in a group – bullies tend to pick on kids who are alone.
- Arrange to meet your child and take her to school if necessary.
- Check that your child is not making herself more vulnerable to being bullied by behaving in a certain way.
- Keep written record of the events that take place.
- If necessary, talk again to the teacher, head teacher, school board and/or the parent/teacher association and ask what is being done to prevent bullying in the school? Do they teach about bullying? Is there a set programme or measures taken if bullying occurs.
- Keep encouraging friendships with other children.
- Encourage your child to take up another hobby to take her mind off the bullying.

Other Steps To Break Bully Group Dynamics

You could suggest that the bullies be kept in school until the other children have gone home. Talk with the parents of the bullying children. Ask for programmes in school to discuss bullying and assertiveness training, agreeing on possible solutions about bullying or punishments if bullying is found. Ensure that the school has a strong policy of *not tolerating bullies* and that the children are well aware of it. Check that the school has excellent play supervision and that any bullying that has been noticed is dealt with immediately.

If your child is still having problems after taking all the steps mentioned, *be persistent and insistent.* Identify the *areas where* bullying take place. *Who* does it and *when*, and write it all down.

Organise a self-defence course for your child to help her protect herself and give her confidence. Self-defence will also teach her how to avoid situations of conflict.

At all times make sure that your child knows that none of this is her fault in any way, emphasising out that it is fault of the bully and she is not the only victim.

If necessary, contact the ISPCC Childline 1800 666 666 or

the police. The safety and well being of your child is the most important issue. Move schools if necessary, if you are able to do so.

Finally, if you suspect your child is a bully, discuss it with her calmly, stressing that hurtful and aggressive behaviour is not allowed. Has she a problem? LISTEN carefully. Is it a reaction to something? If you cannot cope, talk to teachers and find out where to get advice.

EVERY TIME WE SIT DOWN FOR A MEAL MY CHILDREN START FIGHTING. WHAT CAN I DO?

O.K. You have worked hard, cooking a nice meal for the family. It is now ready, the table is set and everyone sits down. And then the fighting starts...

'Mum, Peter stuck his elbow into me.' 'No I didn't, she kicked me under the table.' The exchange of comments continues until Mum is drawn in. Mum starts to get upset and irritated. 'Stop it, all of you', she shouts. Is this familiar?

This squabbling is attention-seeking behaviour and it has worked. Mum was upset and ended up being brought into the row. Everyone's meal was upset, but they did succeed in getting all of Mum's attention.

What To Do?
IGNORE – As usual, ignore this squabbling, attention-seeking behaviour as much as possible. Do not get involved unless it looks like real violence will erupt.

LEAVE THE TABLE – Ask them to leave the table and continue the row outside, or leave the table and come back when they are going to act in a civilised way. Whatever you say keep your voice calm but firm.

NOT FAIR – Tell them that they are not being fair to the rest of the family so they can go to their respective rooms and come back when they feel they can enjoy the meals with everyone else.

RESPONSES – Try experimenting with different responses to the rows.

SITTING – You may find different sitting arrangements may work.

HUNGRY – Don't worry about your children having to go without a meal if they leave the table. You will not need to do this regularly. If they go hungry once they may be slow to row next time. Just cover the meal and they may return for it – remember, no snacking allowed.

DISTRACT – Try distracting their attention by asking questions about their day or school or a friend.

IMPROVE – Talk to the older members of the family and enlist their help in making meals times more enjoyable. How can they help to improve the behaviour of their younger siblings?

LIMITED CHOICE – Try giving a limited choice, such as, 'You can stay at the table if you stop arguing or take your meal into kitchen and eat alone there'.

HELPFUL – Get them all to participate in preparing the meal so that they see how much effort goes into making it. By feeling helpful, useful and busy, they will be less inclined to fight.

DISCUSSIONS – Start discussions on interesting topics

during the meal, so that meal times are fun times to be enjoyed together, times when you will sit and listen to them – if they behave well.

CONSEQUENCES – Instead of reacting to the row, talk to them about what the logical consequence of their fighting behaviour will be. Do they want to end up hungry in their rooms or not? The choice is theirs. Then go off the subject and talk about a different topic.

CHANGES – Think of a different way to have the meals. For example, feed the younger children earlier and let the older ones eat their main meal at school. Leave out easy food that they can prepare themselves for supper later on. Then have set, regular family meals at weekends where everyone makes the effort to have an enjoyable meal with all the trimmings, flowers, napkins etc.

IDEAS – At your next weekly family meeting, ask them for their ideas on ways of making meal times happier.

ENJOYABLE – As a parent, you have the right to eat an enjoyable meal. Enforce that right. Tell them you have that right and insist on it, even if it means eating alone as a couple at times.

Remember, especially as children get older, that you cannot force them to obey. You can only win their co-operation. The best way to do this is by respectful communication. So present your problems to them. 'You are making me and the family upset by your bickering at meal times.' 'Do you think it is fair?' 'Can we talk together and see how we could improve things?' After discussing it, ask, 'Are you happy if we try that?' Then discuss what would be the fair consequences if they do not follow through on the plan.

Eating Tips
- Try to stick to regular mealtimes.
- Make the meal as attractive looking as you can.
- Give small portions and they can always ask for more.
- Be flexible – don't force-feed vegetables or meat, give them one alternative.
- Teach children to cook easy recipes from a young age, so that they appreciate the work involved and can give you time off from cooking occasionally.
- If the children start being difficult about meals, keep biscuits, sweets and junk snacks in a locked cupboard. Or just leave treats off the shopping list and stick to main wholesome meals for a while.

HOW DO I HANDLE ANY JEALOUSY OF A NEW BABY?

We have all felt the pangs of jealousy, the green-eyed monster, at some time. But we all have to learn how to control it or it can spoil our relationships and become a destructive force in our lives and to our happiness.

Jealousy in a child can show itself in many ways, including tantrums, hitting the baby, squabbling with each other or becoming more clingy. Whatever way jealousy manifests itself, there are certain steps that you can take to minimise the jealousy and ways in which to handle it.

Prepare For The New Arrival
Prior to the birth involve siblings, letting them feel baby kicking, telling them they will be the big brother or sister and the baby will love them. Be realistic. Let them know what to expect, explaining that the baby may cry, not speak at first and will need time for feeding etc. But encourage their

involvement in the happy occasion and talk about the time when they where in your tummy.

Explain what will happen if Mummy needs to go to hospital, tell them that they will visit you there and you will return home *plus* baby. Encourage as much independence as possible prior to the birth. This will help you later.

After the birth

- Do not be holding the baby when they first see you after the birth. Let the visit be in between feeds, so that you can give them attention.
- The new baby might have a present for each of the children. This impresses the siblings, especially if the little present was just what they wanted. It is also a good idea if they bring a little gift for the baby.
- Encourage them to be 'mother's little helper' but don't expect too much or it will become a chore. Just let them help you as much as they like and praise them, letting them know you appreciate their help.
- Keep to the same family routines as much as possible, to give the siblings security.
- Give the older children special new privileges, like 15 minutes extra stay up time at night, to show that they are more grown up.
- Make an effort to give the other children special one-to-one attention, too. A baby takes up so much time, I know. But try to give them their own time at bath time, for a nighttime story with them alone, or for a chat when baby is sleeping.
- Enlist the help of others. Now is the time that grand-parents, godparents, uncles and aunts could take them out for a special treat.

If Jealousy Arrives...

VISITORS – Encourage visitors to take notice of the older

children, too. You could perhaps ask a child to take the visitor in to look at the baby and tell them all about her.

MATURITY – Acknowledge her maturity. Show by your interactions with her that you value her company, acknowledge her help and love.

REASSURE – Talk with her. Reassure her you still love her very dearly. If she shows signs of jealousy, encourage her to talk about her feelings.

LISTEN – Acknowledge her feelings and realise she is hurting inside. Sharing how she feels will help her feel better. Listen carefully and give her time to speak, giving her your undivided attention.

NEGATIVE FEELINGS – Let her know that you have negative feelings about the baby, too, sometimes. Talk about sleepless nights or crying. Point out that you don't let these feelings overwhelm the love you have and the happiness you feel about the baby most of the time. Explains that people do have positive and negatives feelings at different times.

INSECURITY – Remember that jealousy stems from a feeling of insecurity. Give your child lots of reassurance and love when you see any signs of jealousy.

SHARING – Teach her to share from an earlier age and she will cope better sharing you.

DIFFERENTLY – Be prepared to treat each child differently. One may need lots more hugs, while another may need an extra hour playing with friends and a reassuring smile on her return.

SAY IT – Teach your child to say what she is feeling and why, for example, 'I do not like you playing with the game because you lose the pieces and that breaks my toy.' That is less confrontational than simply saying, 'No, go away'.

OUTLETS – Channel your child's jealousy or anger into other outlets. Release their tension by letting them have a wrestling match, playing a sport or buying them a punch bag.

BAD BEHAVIOUR – Recognise the negative emotions behind any bad behaviour. Don't shout at them and punish them. Try to get them to verbalise their feelings. 'You are very angry with Peter, why? Is there a reason why you feel this way?'

PRIVATE PLACE – Have a special place she can go where the young ones cannot disturb her, her own private place.

HERO – Let them know that they are the younger one's hero. Explain how they can become the little one's teacher, teaching them to smile, talk, play football and read. Praise them for doing so.

PRECAUTION – It is a wise precaution not to leave the baby unattended with another child, especially a jealous one.

HITTING – If your child ever hits the baby, stay calm, be resolutely firm. Get eye-to-eye contact, holding her firmly, and stress that this is not acceptable behaviour at all. Tell her that when she was a baby you never let anyone hurt or harm her, either, saying, 'We all protected you, so now we must all protect the baby.' Get her to apologise later, when she has calmed down.

CURE – The only real cure for jealousy is loving-time and attention from the parents and any others at hand. Ignore any bold, attention-seeking behaviour, but when she is trying to co-operate give her loving, one-to-one attention, and praise any attempts she makes to overcome her jealousy.

SECURITY – Give them a good self-image and family security with safe limits – that way, they should feel so secure that they'll realise that have no need to be jealous of anyone.

MY CHILD SWEARS TOO MUCH / MY YOUNGER SON SOMETIMES SPITS – I HATE IT. HOW SHOULD I REACT WHEN THIS SORT OF THING HAPPENS?

Q

Coping with Annoying Habits/ Disrespectful Behaviour

When dealing with these situations we must go back to our old friend of helping children realise that such behaviour is their *responsibility*, thus allowing them to keep their dignity, while making sure they understand that they have to *live with the consequences of their actions*.

Spitting

With a calm voice say, 'If you want to stay here you cannot spit' or, 'If you really need to spit you can go to the bathroom.'

If Spitting At Someone

Say firmly, 'You can apologise to your brother now' or even, 'You can go to you room until you decide to apologise'. But you may warn her after a time in her room that the *consequences* of her actions may be to wash the car, or a chore of your choice, if she does not apologise.

Swearing

This is slightly different because there are various reasons why a child may swear. So before you act, think why. Was it to impress her pals, for revenge or because she knows that you'd react? Was it for attention, for a laugh or simply to see what happens? Depending on the reason for the swearing, you may choose to act differently at certain times.

Some of the things you may choose to do...

IGNORE – If it happens only occasionally, you may choose to *ignore* the word. Certainly it would not be wise to make a big issue of it and get upset, as it may cause her to use it to manipulate you at a later date.

QUIET WORD – Say nothing in front of her friends but have a quiet word when they leave. Point out that you do not swear in the home, saying, 'I find it disrespectful, if everyone swore in the home it would be terrible.' Give her a choice – tell her to try not to swear again or you will make it a definite rule, and then she will have to live with the consequences.

SWEAR BOX – If the swearing continues, bring it up at the family meeting. Make it a rule to discuss what the family feels about swearing and what is considered an adequate punishment for breaking the rules. Perhaps a swear box? €1 for adults, 50cent for children, with the money collected being given to charity.

Whatever the annoying behaviour is that you want to stop, remember that it is best not to correct on the spot, instead postponing the talk of choices and consequences until later, when you are both calm. Listen to what she has to say first, as this will give you time to think up the choices that you are going to give her... and the consequences of not complying.

You may think that you are being soft on discipline when giving choices, waiting for the right moment and discussing issues. In fact, the opposite of this is true – it is easy to shout and force, and very difficult to stay calm and evaluate in times of stress. You must be strong enough to follow through on what you say will happen ... being consistent can be tough. Staying in control is the hardest thing to do in times of tiredness and stress. Shouting and hitting are the easy options.

Your Son Talks To You Very Rudely – What Should You Do?

Firstly, ignore the rude behaviour. To be ignored is the natural consequence of being treated without respect. At a later stage you should explain how you were upset by the behaviour and intimate that he should show the same respect shown to him. Give him a choice if it happens again.

Whatever difficulty you may be having with your child, think carefully about what the problem is and what may be at the root of the problem. Then adapt and apply these basic ideas to your own particular child and situation.

1. Consider the situation. What are the CHOICES you could give and what should be the natural CONSE-QUENCES. Then ACT. Do not moan or complain, just do it, and your child will learn that we all have to live with the consequences of what we do and say. Not every idea will work for you. But in trying different steps, methods and ways, you may come up with the perfect solution to a particular difficulty in your family.

2. Always remember to LISTEN first, keep your voice CALM and respectful. You do not have to shout to get the message across and keep aggression out of your voice. This can be hard to do if you have been treated rudely, and that's why you should pick a calm time for any DISCUSSION. Otherwise all parties could get over-heated and it is best to keep discussions friendly.

CHAPTER 3

12 + – The Changing Times

MY DAUGHTER IS ALWAYS PUTTING HERSELF DOWN

Being Sensitively Reassuring

This is a sensitive issue and as parents, we must use all our active LISTENING skills to find out what is at the bottom of the daughter's feelings of inadequacy.

For example, why does she feel that way about herself? Is there anything that we do that compounds further how she feels about herself? Look objectively at how we treat her. Is she looking for attention?

Often a well-meaning parent may console, take pity or even criticise or take over for a child who behaves in this way. Yet all of these reactions reinforce her feelings of inadequacy. All of these reactions reward the way she is behaving.

Instead it is important to show understanding. LISTEN to how she feels but let her 'get on with it,' while at the same time pointing out all the good attributes she has and all the wonderful things she can do. Encourage her attempts at improvement and the development of her interests.

If we try to ignore the 'putting down' and this 'giving up' behaviour, it is not that we do not care but that we can show our caring in another way and time. By not to bringing attention to the behaviour, the moaning does not work.

Children may feel discouraged and bad about themselves from time to time. They are confused and often just need someone to talk to who will be encouraging. So don't criticise. Listen to yourself. Do you only take notice of your daughter when she has done something wrong? Do you pick little faults?

Give good attention at the happy times. Encourage and praise her when she co-operates, tries hard at doing something. Create a home where children are praised for all their efforts. Encourage her to be independent. Encourage a hobby or voluntary work to bolster her confidence.

Let her know it is OK to be just who she is. And let her know that you are there to support her. This will give her loads of confidence. Give her lots of opportunities to make decisions for herself and to take responsibility. We learn in doing and it builds our confidence in ourselves. Failing at something does not make us failures. Failures are the mistakes we learn from.

Respect her feelings and say something like, 'You sound very unhappy with yourself. Do you want to talk about it?' Then give encouraging suggestions but remember that the emphasis should be on listening, without tolerating just 'put down' talk. Treat her as if she is very special and she will believe it. Respect her individuality and do not compare or criticise, allow her to be herself.

Finally, give her a good example of a person who has good self-worth! (see Encouraging Self Worth, p. 74)

MY HUSBAND AND CHILD SEEM TO BE IN A POWER STRUGGLE AND ARE ARGUING A LOT

Preventing Power Contests
It takes two to have a power struggle, so one of the first things you must recognise is that parents should not allow themselves to be drawn into one. It sounds simple but is difficult to do.

How To Prevent Power Struggles
A child defiantly refuses to do as he is told and the father insists on obedience. An angry scene develops – a power struggle has commenced. Here we are back to the way we talk to our children again. (see My son answers back, p. 64)

For example, could this be the scenario? 'Don't just sit there like a lazy lump. Help your mother clear the table,' father says snappily. 'Do it yourself,' says Johnny. 'Don't speak to me like that,' father replies.

No one likes to be talked to in this manner. It can escalate into a battle where neither wants to back down and both want to 'win'. However, there is no winner in this battle of words because, once it starts, both sides lose. That's because whoever 'wins', it will only make the relationship worse in the long term.

If you are the other parent watching this, you could try to nip it in the bud and intervene by distracting their attention, diverting their minds to something else.

Alternatively, the parent involved at the onset should ask politely, 'Could you help me to clear the table please, Son?' Asked in this manner, the son will be less likely to answer back aggressively. He may still not help but at least a battle of words has not commenced. If the father were angry, it would be better for him to leave the room and talk about the situation later, along with other related issues such as chores in the home, responsibilities and needs. This means that every one in the family has to share in helping each other. Alternatively, parents may decide to allot specific chores to each child in an organised way.

During this talk, maintain a respectful manner and tone. Ask how he feels about the general chores around the home and if he feels it is fair that we (the parents) feel he should help out? After listening to his views, communicate your own in a respectful, friendly manner. Next time help is asked for, it will most probably be given. And because you behaved in a reasonable manner, he will generally follow suit. Remember that it is very important that you do have the discussion later on. Otherwise he'll feel that he has just got away without helping and will try it again.

When a parent is angry and feels like shouting at his/her child, the parent should try to stand back and ask, 'Why am I so angry? Is it really the child I am angry with? If I shout, will it improve matters?' The answer is nearly always no!

It is very easy for a parent to be drawn into children's

power struggles, too. 'Mum, David kicked me under the table,' says Darina.'No I didn't but I will, little Liar.' Hassled Mum replies, 'Stop that the two of you. Did you kick her, David?' To which he says, 'No, she's a little liar, but she'll get away with it as usual because she's the youngest, bitch.' And on it could go.

These children certainly know how to get Mum's attention and to bring her in on a power struggle row. Poor Mum is doing her best, but gets needlessly drawn in, time and again. She takes the bait constantly.

Things To Consider...
WHY – The question is why did they behave badly in the first place? Did they want attention? Or want to seek power over the others? Was it for revenge or where they even seeking the approval of another?

REASON – Whatever the reason do not give attention when it is demanded by bold behaviour. Ignore the behaviour until you really feel someone may get hurt. Then separate and isolate, so that you are not giving them whatever they sought by behaving boldly.

LOVING CHAT – If either parent, whether mother or father, feels that they or their partner has a problem then a loving chat is in order. This may happen in a family when a parent and child are of similar temperament. There should be no blame attached but just work out a solution together. Be very tactful how you approach this issue, in a calm frame of mind at a restful moment.

CHANGE – Changing the pattern of how we react is also a good step in lessening any power struggle Next time Johnny makes a nasty comment to his father it may be a good idea for Dad to try a totally different approach from usual. A humorous comment or a joke could even be appropriate to defuse tension.

CRITICISM – Does the parent involved feel he/she is being critical of the son? Do they always start arguing if in each other's company for long? If so, the parent involved should make a positive effort to change the pattern, perhaps something as simple as saying something encouraging each time he/she feels like making a criticism.

ENCOURAGING – Think of all the conversations you have had with your son on that or the previous day. How many were critical? How many were positively encouraging and praising? No one likes to be talked down to, so look at the way you talk to your children on a regular basis.

POSITIVE EFFORT – If a relationship is going through a bad patch, it is up to the adult/parent to make a positive effort to resolve it. Find time to be with that child. If ever a problem arises between parent and child, the best way to resolve it is by giving the child positive time and loving attention. That does not mean letting them away with any 'not helpful' or 'bold' behaviour. You should not do anything for a child that she can happily do for herself.

COMMUNICATION – Remember that the parent who communicates openly will gain the respect of and get more co-operation from the child than the parent who tries to win battles by having shouting matches.

MY TEENAGE DAUGHTER HAS CHANGED SO MUCH. SHE WAS GREAT, NOW SHE IS MOODY, SELFISH AND REBELLIOUS – WHERE DID WE GO WRONG?

Our Approach To The Teens
Teen years are a very challenging time for both parents and child. The teenager is going through big changes, physically

and emotionally. Striving for independence, yet fearful of having it. The parents are anxious, wanting their teenager to be independent but fearing the pitfalls and temptations that such independence could lead to. One attitude or approach will not suit all families but here are some ideas and suggestions that may help the parent and child/adult to get through the teens more easily and happily together.

Suggestions For Handling Teens

Put yourself in her shoes by trying to remember what it was like when your body was developing. Think about how self-conscious you were at the time, how much you wanted to be accepted, how you needed the approval of others and how you loved being encouraged and praised.

A girl can have mood swings at the start of her menstrual cycle. Having to learn how to cope with a monthly bleed, the spots that can erupt on your face, the messiness of the whole thing, not to mention the pain it may cause – let's be honest, periods can be a nuisance... yes, I have read *The Woman's Room*, but I still think they can be annoying! Empathise with your daughter, tell her how you felt and coped with it all.

Teach her about her general well being, explaining that it is advisable to eat small meals regularly and cut down on junk food, as this will keep the blood sugar levels more stable. This in turn will lessen the occurrence of mood swings.

Keep communicating lovingly with your teenager, by actions and words. Teenagers can find it difficult to demonstrate their emotions, getting embarrassed easily. Don't forget to give them a loving hug and tell them you love them, too – even if you get pushed away with a, 'Hey Mum, get lost'.

Remember that love can be shown in many ways. You may have to show you care by saying, 'No, you cannot go to that unsupervised party because there may be drugs or anything could happen and I love you enough to care for your safety.' Your teenager may resent it but talking about it in a friendly way and explaining the reasons for your decisions will show her that you care.

During these teen years, we may find that all our values and standards come under attack from this child for whom we have done our very best since birth. That can feel very hurtful. It may be that some parents may feel resentful or need to behave in an authoritarian way, trying to force or impose their will on these budding adults, flexing their parental muscles. This can damage a relationship. Trying to win their co-operation in a positive way is much more productive.

Your teenager may act like a child at times yet expects to be treated as an adult. This is the most common complaint of all teenagers about their parents, 'They treat me like a child.' It is this balancing act that the parents of a teenager must strive to get right, to give the child/adult enough independence to mature gradually. Generally, the more she is treated like an adult and respected the more she will act like one. But there will be mistakes made – remember this is what they learn from. It is up to you to be hovering in a supportive way in the background, making sure these mistakes are little ones.

Some Tips

SELF-CONTROL – The ideal situation is to guide a child from family control to inner self-control, month by month giving a little more responsibility.

COMPROMISES – To lay down the law to a teenager is asking for a rebellion and a lot of resentment. Develop non-judgmental listening, really trying to understand her point of view and coming to compromises that will not put her in any danger but will help her grow more responsible.

GUIDANCE – Most adolescents need to feel they have a secure family background in which they are loved and parents who are trying to understand her and her views. She does not want

99

to be told what to do, to be criticised for her dress sense and/or her friends, to be lectured to or to have her language complained about. Instead, it is so important to just talk with her in a respectful way to guide her. Most teens will respond positively to loving guidance and the parent taking the lead in the family home. But the teenager tends to rebel against the parent who tries to be boss. Do you see the difference?

EMOTIONS – The teenager must learn to control emotions for herself instead of being a slave to them. We should be there to offer support, enabling her to reach this maturity. We should not be in conflict with her because her emotions at times seem like a turbulent sea. Yes, they may annoy us but we should take time to listen to what she is going through and, as necessary, explain why she may feel like this and how she can help herself get though it.

SYMPATHETIC – Remember that you will get better results from teenagers (and everyone else, for that matter) if you are sympathetic, understanding and mannerly; are willing to help and willing to listen; and, when you are wrong, to admit it. If you feel in the right, put your view across a calmly as possible.

MY CHILD IS DOING EXAMS SOON. HAVE YOU ANY TIPS ON HOW TO HELP HER COPE WITH THE STUDYING AND THE STRESS OF EXAMS?

There is no magic secret to doing well in exams but studying intelligently and efficiently as part of a routine helps. It is important to motivate your child into the habit of regular study at an early age.

I have broken up my study plan into two sections, one for the student and one for the parents.

Study Plan For The Student

HABIT – Persuade her to stop worrying and just start routinely studying every day until it becomes a habit.

LISTEN – Advise her to listen carefully to each teacher in class, so she knows what is expected of her.

WRITE THINGS DOWN – Get her to keep a specific homework book and a revision plan notebook or timetable. Just trying to remember what she needs to cover will not do. Page numbers and important instructions can be forgotten, or information confused.

REVISION – Revision is an essential part of homework, and even if specific homework is not given, a revision plan is essential. Her revision timetable plan should be made out showing subjects to be revised after homework each night. She should ask you or a teacher if she needs help in making this plan to ensure she has covered all the subjects completely.

CHECK – It is a good idea for her to have two copies of the revision timetable plan so she can keep one at home and one at school. Encourage her to check the revision timetable plan to ensure that she has all the books she needs for revision and homework with her.

QUESTIONS – Ask her to write down 2 or 3 specific questions to guide her revision. Old exam papers can help.

STUDY – The first year secondary student should aim to study 1½ hours nightly, moving on to 2 hours and more when exams times come closer. If one night's homework is heavy going and her time runs out, she can complete her revision plan on a night when the homework is lighter or at the weekend.

SUMMARY SHEETS – Suggest that she composes 'summary sheets' of the main points from each subject to help her revise quickly towards the end.

USE ANY FREE PERIODS WISELY – Let's face, it nearly every week our children get free periods for one thing or another. These free periods should be utilised. Suggest that she gets her homework started or go through her revision plan. This will give her more free time at home.

EARLY – Remember that study done as early in the night as possible tends to be better absorbed, as we all get tired as the evening wears on and therefore less efficient.

BEST TIMES – Get her to work out when is the best time for her to study, remembering that some work great in the morning, others are night owls. Encourage her to find out her best times and how she prefers to study. In short blasts or in long stretches at high levels of concentration? Does she study better alone or with a friend? Let her do what suits her personally.

COSY SPOT – Create a cosy spot where she likes to study. A quiet, well lit place away from family distractions like TV, radio and music. It is up to you, her parent, to tell everyone not to disturb her, especially when high levels of concentration are needed. She can always phone friends back later.

PLAN – Suggest that she plans out how she's going to tackle each subject for revision and the time involved. It is generally better to start with the easy part and giving longer time for the difficult one later. Her plan should be user-friendly, with summary notes, headings, highlighting important bits and making revision cards. Get her to use key words to jolt her memory.

PRACTISE – She should test herself under exam conditions at home to practise. This is a good way to test memory recall. If she experiences difficulties, she can look up the question later.

PAMPER – Remember to encourage her to eat and sleep well. This is very important. This is an important time for her, so she should be good to herself and pamper herself a little. When she has done her study time, she can reward herself for a job well done!

DON'TS

- Don't let her leave studying to the last minute. Or try to stay up all night before the exam, cramming.
- Don't let her avoid the subjects she dislikes or finds difficult.
- Don't let her forget that there is a life after exams.

Preparing For The Exam Itself

Encourage her to …

- Get up in plenty of time, giving herself plenty of time to get to school and the specified exam room.
- Check she has all she needs for the exam such as extra pens, pencils, ruler, coloured crayons, tissues, a drink… is there anything else she specifically needs?
- Make sure she knows what exam she is taking and where it is being held.
- Go to the toilet beforehand.
- If she has butterflies in her tummy, suggest relaxation or breathing techniques. Tell her to breathe slowly, stay calm and say calming words inside her head, like 'peace'.
- Read the instructions carefully when she gets the exam paper and to ask the teacher if anything is unclear.
- Read all the questions, more than once if needs be. Advise her to give herself a set time for each question and to plan how much time she can give to each part,

underlining the key words in the question to make sure she sticks to the point.

- Write down at the top the time she should finish or the time allowed for each question to remind her to stop, so she doesn't get carried away.
- Go on to the next question, if she gets stuck. She can come back to it later if she has finished the paper. If she is still stuck, give an intelligent guess – why not?
- If possible, leave time to read through and check her answers.
- Not to panic whatever happens. If she feels stressed out, suggest that she talk to someone about her feelings, perhaps you as her parents, teachers, friends, even the Childline 1800 666 666 (Ireland) – see your local phone book for your number.
- When finished, to put it out of her mind and enjoy herself – she gave it her best shot and cannot ask more of herself than that.

Study Plan For Parents

Start off my making sure that there is a special area in your home that is for study that is well lit, comfortable and with no distractions. Then make a point of looking over homework. Help the child assess how long the work takes, and show you are interested. The older child may not need this but take an encouraging interest.

SUPPLIES – Remember to buy in extra supplies of all necessary items. Pens, pencils, rubbers, rulers, sharpeners etc., plenty of time ahead of the exams.

ENCOURAGEMENT – Give plenty of encouragement, not pressure.

SUPPORT – Give support not criticism. Relax your home rules a little. Whilst studying she should not have to help with the house chores.

ROUTINE – Make it easy for your child to study as a routine in the family home.

NUTRITION – Teenagers especially have enormous nutritional needs and appetites. Give regular meals and small regular snacks to keep her going. This will keep the blood sugar level up and aid concentration. Avoid junk food and give fruit juices and nutritious snacks. Pamper her a little, doing the things you would not normally do as a little treat.

BEHAVIOUR – It is best not to comment on behaviour such as not having a shower, staying up late or being a little irritable. Forget it, they'll get back to normal after the exams.

RELAXATON – Teach your child relaxation techniques to help her out if she feels stressed.

BREAKS – Make sure she gets regular breaks for food and fresh and exercise. Mum coming in with an encouraging word, milk and a sandwich, will liven up flagging spirits.

VITAMINS – It is an idea to give a course of multi-vitamins and minerals in the months coming up to exams, to ensure that all her nutritional requirements are catered for.

PERSPECTIVE – Finally, parents should keep things in perspective. It is only an exam – if you are worried get advice from a teacher.

UNITED FRONT – If you are a two-parent family, talk to your partner about the approach to the exams to give a united front.

CARD – Buy a fancy little card to her taste and in it let her know that you realise she is trying her best and that you'll love her, whatever happens.

BE THERE – Make sure that you are around during this stressful time. Do extra things for her, like driving her to school, doing lunches, and just being there to talk to – this all helps the student a lot.

MY CHILD REFUSES TO DISCUSS ANYTHING, SHE JUST SHUTS UP AND WON'T TALK!

Encouraging Communication

Speak to her in a respectful tone, not in a critical or sarcastic way. Remember that when you use the word 'you' a lot, it tends to sound hostile. By using 'I' instead, you are taking responsibility for the feelings instead of blaming the other.

Do not call her names like lazy, mean, bully or stupid. These names can hurt deeply and stick inside a child's mind and could label her for a long time. Think through the day of your conversations with your child. How many nice conversations have you had? How many critical ones? How many times did you just keep asking questions or giving instructions?

Make sure you have positive talks with her… not just telling her what to do, but normal conversations. Go out of your way to have a chat, encourage her to talk and share with her, about anything, her hobby, football, a book, something you know she is interested in.

If necessary, suggest a walk, an outing or something you can both do together, where the talk can take place casually.

Listen

Here are a few ways to improve you listening skills…

• Pay attention. Get contact with her eyes and perhaps by touching, if you feel it is the right time. Do try not to do other things, instead give her your full attention.

- Don't do very much speaking yourself; just listen. When you do speak, keep it short, supportively encouraging her to say more, perhaps by repeating what she says again. 'You find it hard at school – is that what you're saying?' Or leading her to say more by saying, 'Is that what you mean?' or 'You seem unhappy about that' or 'What if?' and 'Why?' Or stay just nodding or smiling.
- Try to really understand how she is feeling. Can you remember how it felt to be that age? Can you talk to her about your past?
- Let her know you enjoy talking with her. Enjoy her and her company. Tell a few jokes together.

Whatever has happened to stop the communication between father and son, it is up to the father to make positive moves to re-establish communication and the sooner the better for everyone. The father is the adult and the son is only learning to be one.

Remember, too, that to apologise when we are in the wrong is a good example to give and gains respect from all those around us.

It is very important to keep the lines of communication open during the teen years – they still need your friendship and guidance, they just don't want to be seen to want it.

MY DAUGHTER IS SMOKING AND I HATE IT

Teaching Children to Look after Themselves and to Consider the Feelings of Others

If we are to educate our children about the evils of smoking, we must first know them ourselves. It was not until the 1950s that the medical profession first realised the link between smoking and lung cancer. Since then the message has got louder and louder.

SMOKING KILLS YOU but not before it generally gives you a life of suffering. It causes not only lung cancer but also mouth and throat cancer. It goes in through the mouth and all around your body and then even when you go to the toilet it follows you so you can even get cancer in the bladder.

But cancer is not the only disease that SMOKING is linked to – it causes many other diseases such as heart disease, lung problems and peptic ulcers. The manufacturers argue that people don't have to smoke if they do not want to – this is rubbish! Seventy per cent of smokers do want to give it up but find it difficult because they are ADDICTED.

90 % of people start smoking when they are children.

It is said that during children's rebellious years, they first reach for sweets and the next step is cigarettes. A Prof. Moxhams once said, 'In the gap between bubble gum and sex there is one irresistibly attractive taboo – tobacco!' Unbelievably 25% of our children have taken up smoking by the time they are 16 years old.

Our children are confronted every day with images of people who smoke in the shops, on TV, at school. These images may often contradict the message of 'no smoking' that we have tried to encourage in our home.

In the face of all of this what can we parents do to stop our children from smoking?

How Can We Help Prevent Our Children From Smoking?

My first suggestion could be the hardest for many parents. DO NOT SMOKE YOURSELF. The child of a smoker is more likely to get asthmatic attacks, serious chest infections, glue ear, and is more likely to be off school because of ill health. We inhale 15% of a cigarette; the other 85% is second-hand smoke that is passed on to be taken in passively by others around us.

By giving up smoking you increase your child's chances of being a non-smoker and having a healthier life. It is not easy but it can be done with help. Contact your GP or your CANCER SOCIETY for advice on support groups and leaflets and remedies that may aid you.

Other ways to help your children...

1. Make Your Home A Smoke-Free Zone
2. If this is not possible, have a smoking room only, one that is rarely used by the children of the home.
3. If you have a baby-sitter, employ a non-smoker or one who does not smoke around your children.
4. Avoid smoking in the car or using the smoking areas on public transport or restaurants etc.
5. Discuss openly in your home in a non-confrontational manner, the evils and effects of smoking long term. Discuss any family or friends that smoke, why, what it does to their health? Do not be authoritarian about this so they rebel and want to smoke. Explain to them gently the problems attached to smoking in a caring way. That way the door is open for them to come to you if they are tempted or have even started to smoke, and you can help them prevent addiction.
6. Consider offering an incentive like giving them €100 at the age of 21 if they are not smokers ... they are unlikely to take it up after that. I know one family of seven where this worked well; they are all non-smokers and all better off by much more than the €100, financially as well as health wise!

'Uncool'

Talk about smoking in a very negative, `uncool' way, so that they are not tempted to glamorise smoking at all. If you go into an area where someone has been smoking, comment on the nasty smell of smoke. Point out the other nasty side effects of smoking such as BAD BREATH, YELLOW STAINED

TEETH and WRINKLES … smoking really ages your skin. Educate in a positive way against smoking at all times.

Young girls watching their weight may excuse their smoking as a means of not putting on weight. This really upsets me. They watch the stick models and want to copy them. The only way to deal with this is to point out the models and famous people in the media, and teach them how to deal with the so-called glamorous world. Urge them to look at these people's real lives and show that all that glitters certainly is not gold. Happiness comes from inside, not out.

If young girls want to stay slim, fine. Exercise keeps your body weight down, while improving muscle tone, strength, stamina and mental awareness. Regular physical activity relieves stress, controls weight and is conducive to avoiding smoking and helps you look younger. Unlike smoking, which causes wrinkles. So encourage any exercise your child is inclined to.

Already Smoking?

If you have already discovered that you have a child who has started to smoke, say you would like to have a chat about her smoking at a quiet moment.
Then…

LISTEN – to what she has to say. Does she smoke because she wants to be IN with friends? Because she wants to be skinny? WHY?

NOT FAIR – Present your point of view. Point out that her smoking is not fair to the rest of the family; talk about passive smoking, bad example and bad for her health, etc.

SOLUTIONS – Think up solutions together. Let her think of them first. Guide her but try to let her find an alternative for herself. For example, that she smokes only in the garden or keeps it to social smoking with friends outside the home or perhaps doesn't smoke in anyone's company. Or whatever you both come up with. Hopefully you will get support leaflets together.

INCENTIVE – Give an incentive for her to give up smoking, a special something she has always wanted, such as a Walkman, a holiday or joining a gym together. Think up a plan / solutions together and make them work.

SUPPORT – There is no point in rowing over smoking, as the person must want to give up and needs help and support, not criticism.

Remember that every day thousands of innocent young children have no choice but to breathe in second-hand smoke – make sure it is not yours! All of us should claim our right to live and breathe clean air, so we can lead healthy lives.

CHAPTER 4

Specific Situations

 I FEEL LIKE A SLAVE IN MY OWN HOME. HOW CAN I GET MY CHILDREN TO HELP ME?

I think most parents, especially mothers, have times like this when they feel that a general dogsbody. It can lead to being disheartened, feelings of 'being used' and resentment – no one likes to feel this way. It is also definitely not fair if one or two people in a household are left to do all the work. So what do we do about these feelings and importantly, how do we stop ourselves being used in this manner?

What To Do?

Firstly, if ever you have any negative feelings, accept them and do something about them, for example leave the house, have a walk and decide what steps to take.

Decide how you want to deal with this problem without nagging, scolding or criticising. Think about how staying calm can you get your children's co-operation. Is it one child or are all the family not 'pulling their weight?'

During a family meeting or a one-to-one when everyone is calm, explain to the family how you feel and why – not in an aggressive tone, but in a sensitive manner. Be careful how you word it; use the word 'I' rather than 'you', which sounds like blame. 'I really get upset when I go into your bedroom and have to pick up all the clothes every day. Can you under-stand why I feel this way?' Encourage them to see your point of view clearly. Keep your tone and voice friendly. Ask for suggestions to alleviate the problem. LISTEN to what the child has to say.

Alternatively, have a family agreement, or a contract between the children and you as to what chores each one does. Pin it up in the kitchen for all to see. Make sure all are in agreement. All could sign it if you want to.

A principle all parents should remember is not to do too much for a child. If we constantly do things for them, how do they ever learn? If we do everything for them how are they supposed to learn confidence? If we do too much for them how are they going to develop their own self-worth or discover all the natural consequences of their own actions or lack of them? Thus it is actually better for them in NOT doing something for them sometimes.

Before putting this principle into practice we must be careful about what we expect of our children.

Expectations

PHYSICALLY – Firstly make sure your children can physically do what you are asking of them. For example, don't get them to put their clothes away if they can't reach the hangers.

TEACH – Do not expect them to do things like hanging out the washing if you have not first taught them the correct way to do it.

STANDARDS – Do lower your standards where appropriate. A 9 year old will not make a bed in the same way as you. Accept this and praise the effort. The older they get the better the effort expected, so in a joking or friendly way mention that only half of the dishes have been put away.

SPECIFIC JOBS – Even if you like housework or are lucky enough to have someone to help you do housework, do have specific jobs for which your children take responsibility. Otherwise the basic daily living tasks like cooking, cleaning and laundry, which they will need in later life, will not be taught. It does give great satisfaction to a child knowing she contributes to the running of the home.

ENJOYMENT – Remember that in addition to the everyday chores, there are some jobs around the home that children will actively enjoy. The job list could include tasks like sorting out old family photos into albums and time sequence; washing the car; tidying big cupboards or wardrobes; helping at children's parties; and organising toy boxes.

POCKET MONEY – A word about pocket money. The value of money needs to be learned. One way to do this is by giving money weekly, provided chores are done. It hopefully teaches our children to be good managers of money. Agree on a reasonable amount weekly, although a special task/job may well deserve a bonus. Do encourage them to save for big items or for holidays.

The above ideas are helpful in encouraging children, as they grow older, to do their fair share in the running of the family household, as well as giving them more responsibility and practice on how to run their own homes in the future. The absolute natural consequences for the older child of not helping or contributing to the running of the household is to be asked to move out and run her own home, if old enough. Any consequences like this for the over 18s should be discussed in a friendly manner, as they need to learn what are the results of their decision not to co-operate. In life we need to look after ourselves and co-operate with those around us, whether that is at home, at school or at work.

So if YOU have a problem ...

- State how you feel, using 'I', and present your point of view in a friendly way.
- Listen to their views and reactions, keep calm and use the right tone in the discussion.
- Can they think of ways to improve the situation?
- Agree on some settlement that encourages help, compromise and co-operation for all. Write down the agreement or plan and make sure everyone knows the consequences of breaking the agreement.
- Remember that nagging, scolding and rowing tend not to encourage co-operation but can be counter-productive for all.

Doing things this way should ...

1. Encourage your children to think and hopefully teach them to consider others and *their* feelings.
2. Give your children a choice of helping / contributing or not.
3. Teach them to live with the consequences of their

actions. This is where it is important for PARENTS to have limits and rules and to stick to them, so that children learn from the consequences of their own actions.

4. Win a teenager's co-operation rather than forcing her to do something, thus developing natural mutual respect.
5. Encourage self-discipline.

MY CHILD SEEMS TO HAVE LEARNING PROBLEMS

How To Cope With Learning Difficulties

Many children start to show signs of having a learning problem from a very early age.

Perhaps some may be slow to talk or have developmental delays. Or they display difficulties in reading in their early school years. Any of these may go unrecognised. Sometimes the learning problems may not even be picked up until the teenage years. If this sounds like your child, there is hope. There are many learning problems that can occur but there are things that we as parents can do to help our children help themselves at whatever age.

The Problem

Identify the particular learning problem your child has by going to the experts. Research has shown that learning problems are due to difficulties with the way the brain handles information. In short that means that even though your child is really trying her best to read, she may be experiencing problems. By identifying which problem she has, we can then use different skills to overcome them, directing the talents they have to the right field.

A good example of a person with learning problems

triumphing over his learning disabilities is Albert Einstein, who was probably dyslexic and dysgraphic yet overcame them to become a world famous scientist.

A child with a learning problem may be very bright or be of average intelligence. But sometimes they are labelled wrongly as lazy, slow or not trying their best, when really they have difficulties, for example knowing how letters make up words or how words expressed in a sentence make sense.

What Causes The Problem?

No easy answer here. It can be one complicated reason or a combination of several reasons. Some inherited condition or illness may affect baby when in the mother's womb. But for the most part, we do not know all the answers yet. People are complicated, fantastic beings and sometimes we do not know why something in the mechanisms of our learning abilities may go wrong.

Some Early Signs Of A Learning Problem

- If your child fails to follow directions and appears to forget things almost immediately after you have spoken.
- If your child seems to be a daydreamer, or taking a long time to finish a simple task.
- If your child has problems organising work at school or home.
- If your child has a difficulty grasping any particular subject. Or seems slow at the basic reading, writing or arithmetic.

It is always best to acknowledging any budding learning problem as soon as possible so it can be identified and then dealt with. Remember that the learning problem may be difficult to recognise at first and the child appears normal. And of course the child is normal but may have a learning problem and needs all the help they can get to overcome it. Contact your GP, teachers, health and educational professionals in this field who can identify and suggest ways to help this particular problem.

Types Of Learning Problems

(1) DYSLEXIA – is basically a problem with reading. The child can have difficulties with words, letters, sentences and paragraphs. However, because of this difficulty it can affect the child in very many and varied ways. It is not a visual problem but the way in which the brain interprets the information it is given.

(2) DYSGRAPHIA – is a learning problem with writing. The child may have difficulty in spacing and forming letters correctly. Despite an enormous effort from the child, handwriting may be very time consuming and hard to read. Teachers may complain written work is never finished on time. Or copying work from the blackboard is very difficult for them in the time given. Again, the problem is how the brain interprets what it 'sees'.

(3) DYSCALCULIA – is the term given for a child with a problem with mathematics. She may do well in other subjects but have a problem with numbers. This can be very frustrating for the teacher, parents and especially for the child.

(4) AUDITORY MEMORY AND PROCESSING PROBLEM – is a big name for the child with a problem with remembering and understanding sounds. Again, it usually nothing to do with hearing but the way the brain interprets the words and sounds.

(5) Some children may even have a mixture or combination of the above problems.

What Can A Parent Do?

DIAGNOSIS – Seek early diagnosis of particular problem.

STRENGTHS – Build on your child's other strengths. For example, if maths is a problem, develop a love of reading and writing. If writing is a problem, develop interests using their hands, or music. Explore new strengths and introduce new challenges for them that use other skills so they can build their self-confidence.

CHOICE – Discuss at length the choice of subjects and work at developing your child's strengths rather than weaknesses. Make wise education and career choices, armed with all the facts about your particular child. Talk to guidance counsellors, teachers, health worker or all involved. It is important that everyone involved in the education of your child is aware of what her particular problem is. Most schools and universities have assistance now for children with learning problems and, once identified, they can be taught skills to deal with problems they come up against.

DIFFICULTIES – Learning difficulties can affect children in many ways. It can cause a child to be shy, withdrawn, rejected by peers, or be angry and be labelled a bold child, when at the bottom of this misunderstood child is someone simply trying to cope with a problem.

SPECIAL HELP – These children may need parents' special help in finding friends, participating in activities and enjoying the company of others in areas where their learning problem plays no part. Scouts, sports, hobbies, mountain climbing, you name it. Encourage participation in something they enjoy that gives them confidence and a good self-esteem.

READ – Read up on your child's particular problem and learn what you can do to specifically help.

SUPPORT – Encourage family support by ensuring that all

the members know about the problem, are sympathetic about it and help in any way they can.

STUDY – Provide a quiet, well-lit study area with minimal distractions.

SELF-IMAGE – Positively promote a good self-image by emphasising and praising her many good assets and skills.

OTHER SKILLS – Work with her to develop any compensatory skills to overcome problems. For example, learning how to type at an early stage if writing is a problem or using tapes if the written word is hard to decipher. Good notes on all subjects are important, so getting the teacher to co-operate giving photocopies on notes or tapes or whatever is necessary for your child to get the information properly interpreted. Practise any necessary skills at home.

SPECIALISTS – Find tutors or a specialist to assist you. Consult with them about setting reasonable goals for your child. Find out all the help that is available for you and her.

EXAMS – Find out what measures can be taken to help her for examinations. For example, could her question to read out to her, if she has trouble with the written word?

COMPUTERS – These can be of great help to a child with learning problems. There are many programmes to aid those with learning difficulties. To learn to use a keyboard is a great asset and should be encouraged.

INFORMATION – There is hope and help available for those with learning difficulties but not enough. Sometimes the information can be difficult to find, but keep at it – there is help out there.

HOW CAN I HELP MY CHILDREN TO COPE WITH THE DEATH OF A LOVED ONE IN THE FAMILY?

Q

Children and Death

When someone in or close to the family dies, it affects the whole family, even the very young child. The effect it has can vary from physical ailments to behavioural difficulties, including the normal emotional upheaval. Death is a sad but inevitable part of everyone's life. Grief is a human emotion we will all feel at some time.

The dictionary defines grief as 'deep or violent sorrow' after someone dies. We can all feel this sorrow, adults and children alike. It is one feeling from which we cannot shield our children. Children's distress after a loved one dies can be devastating and powerful. It can persist and be rekindled over the years, by small things like a father picking up friends at school may remind the child of her own departed Dad.

Yet although death is as intense and overwhelming for a child as an adult, there is plenty of evidence that it may not necessarily be a damaging experience. In fact, if we support and help a child through the trauma of a death it may even help that child grow stronger within herself.

How To Help...

In practical terms children need four things:
- INFORMATION
- TO BE LISTENED TO
- EXTRA LOVING ATTENTION
- TO SEE YOU GRIEVING AND TO BE ALLOWED TO GRIEVE IN THEIR OWN WAY

Information

When you give any information to a child concerning what is

121

happening or has happened, be clear and honest. We all long to protect our children from hurt but evading the truth will not help in the long-term – saying things like, 'Daddy has gone asleep forever,' may trigger a reaction in the child of being terrified to go to bed at night.

Be careful what you say. Let the news about the death be told by someone who is close to the child and preferably at home, where the child feels secure. Be specific, for example. 'Daddy's body has stopped working and they cannot mend it'. Explain that Daddy cannot be hurt, feel cold or be ill any more otherwise the burial or cremation may cause even greater distress to the child. Check back with simple words to make sure the child understands what has happened. Be prepared to answer the same questions repeatedly. This is the child just trying to make sense of it all.

Touch is all-important. Depending on the age or temperament, hold a hand or sit the child on your lap, or take her in your arms. Your loving, caring presence will help the child feel less abandoned.

At different ages and stages of development, children can react very differently. Yet it may be of some comfort to know that there are stages of grief that most children and adults go through.

If a person is dying, let the child decide how much she wants to be involved. If the person is in hospital, it is important that she is allowed to say goodbye – she may want to give a gift like a drawing. Let her stay for as short or as long a time as she wants – even the young child can be aware of her own limitations.

These are the reactions that can occur in response to death:–
- SHOCK – Crying, withdrawn or generally bewildered.
- DENIAL – They just cannot believe it.
- SEARCHING – Naturally it is logical to try to find reasons. They will also be afraid of losing others, too.

- DESPAIR – The crying may start again and there may rejection of other loved ones.
- ANGER – A child may demonstrate aggressive behaviour.
- ANXIETY and GUILT – These may be mixed with DEPRESSION. The child must be able to talk about all these mixed-up emotions.

How Children Of Different Ages React To Death

UNDER 2s – will cry and be distressed at the disappearance of someone they depended upon. However, they will turn to a loving parent-substitute if consistent loving attention is offered.

2 TO 5 AGE GROUP – will not really understand the loss and often keep looking for the loved one, repeatedly asking questions. They may have temper tantrums and develop destructive behaviour. It may help the carer to cope if they understand it is the child's way of coping with the grief. It is better to keep with her usual routines if possible, as this helps the child to feel more secure.

SCHOOL AGE – grieving children may become preoccupied with dying and death. Peers are all-important here, as how friends react to the death may help her cope better – a word or two with her friends' parents may help. There may be an inability to concentrate at school. A feeling of loneliness often afflicts her and she may even blame herself in some way for the death. Encourage the child to attend the funeral but abide by whatever her personal choice is. This child may need you to give her permission to get back into life; she may need you to tell her she can go out and play and be normal again and that is OK.

OVER 10s – encourage her to talk, share and relive the memories of the past and her personal experiences with the deceased. Be there to support and listen; also enlist other members of the family, friends and teacher to be there for support as needed.

TEENAGERS – the death of a loved one can be especially difficult for teenagers, just as they were trying to reach independence. They tend to go either way, attempting to mature too rapidly and try to take the responsibility of the world on their shoulders, or become rebellious and wild. Thankfully, however, some seem to take it all in their stride and manage to come to terms with their loss.

Practical Advice
- Always allow a child to cry. Don't say, 'That's enough' or anything like it, crying is a way of healing the hurt.
- Explain the concept of death in simple terms. Ask the child what they think is happening or what death is?
- Listen carefully if they seem to want to talk or share how they feel with you.
- Be careful not to overwhelm or try to protect them too much.
- Try not to be tempted to whisk the children away; they need to feel this experience to get through it. It is best for them not to be separated from the close family.
- Allow them time to mourn in their own way.
- Help all their efforts to get back to normal; encourage them to go to the disco, if that is what they want to do. Don't make them feel guilty for wanting to get on with normal life. Be happy with them when they want to be happy and be a shoulder to cry on, or cry with them when they want to cry.
- If a child is obviously having difficulties, get professional guidance. Check locally if there is any bereavement counselling service. It may be a good idea for the family to talk over their emotions, even if they are coping well.

I FIND IT SO HARD TO COPE BEING A SINGLE PARENT

Q

Helpful Tips For The Single Parent And How It Can Affect The Children

It is hard enough to bring up children when there are two parents in a family. So being a lone parent is very challenging. There are many reasons why a child is raised in single parent families. Separation, divorce or death gives a parent no option but to be a single parent. It could be the result of an unplanned pregnancy or it can also be a matter of choice. Whatever the reasons, there are certain problems that may occur.

Separation / Divorce

It may be a good idea to get some sort of counselling. The counsellor could offer both you and your child a chance to talk over any problems the changing circumstances cause. Children's reactions to a separation or divorce can vary greatly, depending on their relationship with the parents.

Children tend to have difficulty putting their feelings into words. So many act out how they feel in their behaviour. Having physical feelings like tummy aches or behavioural difficulties is common. For example:–

- The young child could regress to babyish behaviour, bedwetting, have eating problems or tantrums;
- School children are more likely to feel angry, depressed, guilty or just sad; and
- Teenagers may be rebellious and moody, worrying about the possibility of moving home, loss of friends, loss of income. Both the school child and the teenager may suffer a drop in school performance and have more sick leave than usual.

Custody

Problems in this area can cause untold difficulties, if not sorted out well. Stay as friendly as possible with the other parent, no matter how difficult it is. This is best for the children. Co-operation between parents is so important for the child.

The custodial parent tends to look after the child on a day-to-day basis, the other parent perhaps seeing the child on a regular weekend or monthly basis. This does not mean the parent should not remain in close contact with the child. They can still phone, do homework and contribute in any way they can for the good of the child generally. It is usually best for the child if the non-custodial parent keeps in touch and stays involved.

It is important, no matter what access the parents have, that children have ONE place they can call HOME, so that they feel secure and stable. Talk together about how the separation will affect the lives of each parent and each child involved. Remember that your children will usually have loyalties to each parent. Please do not ask them to take sides or involve them in any arguments between you and your partner.

Avoid rowing in front of the children, especially about *them*. Listen to yourself! I know it is hard but try not to criticise your partner in front of the children, even if he/she may have said or done some nasty things to you. Explain that people say and do things that they would not normally do when they are very hurt, angry or sad. They may say them out of hurt, even if they are not true and they do not even believe it themselves. We have all said some things in the heat of the moment that we are sorry for afterwards.

Do not discuss your concerns about the children with your partner in front of them or where they can overhear you. Your children may be confused and upset about 'losing' a parent. *Listen* to how they are feeling about the situation and let them know *you love them*, whatever happens. They may feel alone, unwanted and unloved.

Make sure your children know they are *not responsible* for the situation, as many children blame themselves. Encourage your children to discuss their fears. They may fear you will leave them, too. Be as reassuring as possible.

Finally, despite the pressure that separation and divorce puts on children, the good news is that children can and do recover very well from the trauma of a divorce, and move on to live rewarding, happy lives.

REMEMBER TO TAKE CARE OF YOURSELF – this is a very difficult time for everyone. You may feel anxious and depressed. Look after yourself, get time away from the children. Exercise, take up a hobby, be good to yourself. If you do not treasure yourself and be happy and healthy as you can be, you will not be able to give the support and good example of coping with difficulties to your children.

Survival Tips For Single Parenting

With no one to share the day-to-day responsibilities, caring, and decision-making, single parents can find it very difficult at times. They need to provide greater emotional support and also tend to have a greater financial burden, as well. All this can make a single parent feel very alone at times. So here are some suggestions that any single parent may find useful for daily living.

QUALITY TIME – Even though you may work hard inside and outside the home, try to spend a little time with your child everyday. I know sometimes you may feel exhausted and overwhelmed with all the responsibilities, but try to take time to do something together like an evening short walk, or reading a book or having a chat as you tuck them into bed. There is a knock-on effect if your relationship is good with your child – discipline is easier, they want to help and under- stand more. So it is really worth the effort of giving a little quality time every day.

FEELINGS – Encourage your child to share her feelings. She will cope much better with emotional upsets by sharing them with you. Remember, you do not have all the answers – you cannot change some things. Sometimes it is enough to just listen and give a hug to show you understand.

PROBLEMS – A child who has problems will not just talk about them once and then the problems magically disappear/go away! You may have to 'revisit' a subject a few times, as she tries to understand the issues involved. Be a good listener.

ROUTINE – Provide a daily structure to your child's life and try to keep to a routine. A regular family routine and bedtime will help her feel more relaxed and secure.

PLAN – Make a plan. What can you do to improve your lot? This may mean taking up a hobby, re-training or gaining another work skill. Many job schemes will also help you to find work later on.

FINANCES – Figure out your financial situation. Finances are often a challenge for a single parent and 90% of single parents are women. Work out the cost of your basic needs, including food, clothing, education, recreation, how you are going to get it? Are you getting all you are entitled to?

BUDGET – Learn how to budget your time and money. Know when your income or entitlement money comes in and write down a plan of payments in a budgeting book. Making a list of payments due, when the incoming money is available and when the out going bills can be paid. If in financial difficulties, there are many government programmes to give assistance. Also check the Single Parent Support Groups for any crèches or other help that could be available.

CHILDCARE – Find good childcare. This is easier said then done (see Childcare Options p. 36). If you are a parent working outside the home, it is essential to get this right. The shortage and expense of childcare can make working very difficult for single parents. But do not cut corners here, good childcare is serious and of the utmost importance. Check for any local authority, voluntary crèches or work schemes that assist the single parent.

SUPPORT – Provide emotional support for your child. If you are in a stressful situation, get emotional support for yourself, too. Discuss your concerns with self-help groups, friends, family, anyone you feel may be able to support you. However, be careful not to over-burden your child with your fears or worries. This can be tempting if you have no adult to talk things over with.

LOVE – Explain that every family is different. Some with one parent, some with two. Others with grandparents, others not. Some children may live with people other than their parents. Love is what makes a family special, whatever the size and shape. Don't spend all your time with your children though. You have needs too. They have playtime, so should you.

JOIN – Get to know single parents through support groups, and any other groups that may be of interest, then join!

CHANGE – Avoid worrying about the things you cannot change. Write a list of things you want to change and steps towards reaching your aim.

NOT TOO FAST – Treat your child like children. They have a right to grow up at a normal pace. Don't let any upset make them have to grow up too fast, emotionally.

YOUR TIME – Do something nice for yourself at least once a week, like going to a movie, going on a long walk with a pal, having dinner with a friend.

POSITIVE – Try and keep a positive outlook. If you are separated or divorced, or if a partner has died, remember that the pain will ease in time.

ROLE MODELS – We cannot be both a father and a mother to a child. All children need as many good adult role models as possible. Grandparents, uncles, aunts, friends sisters, brothers neighbours, teachers may all help here.

ENJOY – Take time every day to just enjoy your children.

LIMITATIONS – Understand that you can only do so much. Do not feel guilty about things you can't do or provide because you are not two. You are wonderfully one! We all only have one heart and if it is full of love that is all we and our children need.

SHARE – Realise you are not completely alone. There are people who will help you, just find them and share with them. Find support – there is no such thing as a super parent. Get help where you can!

HOW CAN A PARENT TEACH A CHILD SELF-DISCIPLINE, RIGHT FROM WRONG AND A GOOD SET OF MORAL VALUES?

Encouraging Self-Discipline
Let's face it. We cannot be perfect role models for our children all the time.

The word discipline is sometimes used incorrectly.

Discipline has much more to do with teaching than controlling. More to do with guiding, giving choices and believing the child will make the right decision, and then allowing the child to live with the consequences, even when they may take the wrong road.

The parent who wants to teach self-discipline will not demand obedience and give out punishments for refusing to comply. Instead, that parent will encourage independence, give choices and expect a child to contribute because of mutual respect. Disciplining in this way does not mean 'being soft.' On the contrary, disciplining in this way sets realistic standards, encouraging and focusing on strengths.

Giving choices and letting natural or applied consequences guide a child is very difficult to do. It takes strength of character and being very consistent, following through with any consequences laid down. Self-disciplining tends to be slower than having the rules and punishment system. But teaching the child discipline from within tends to help a child grow in confidence, teaches a child how to make decisions for herself, and helps self-respect and self-confidence grow.

So instead of punishing or shouting at your child for not getting up in the mornings, buy an alarm clock and let her go in late if she does not get up. Don't bail her out but let her live with the consequences of her actions. To encourage self-discipline, we must have GOOD COMMUNICATION with our children. Whilst listening and talking together, the aim is to help our children become responsible adults with respect for themselves and those around them.

Setting Secure Limits

Ideally, start from babyhood and then follow on through the years. Set definite limits and define the consequences of breaking the set limits. With the young, 'NO' can be a knee-jerk reaction from a parent. Try to use other words like 'wait' and use 'no' only occasionally and then say it with conviction, 'NO'. This prepares them to set limits for themselves as they mature.

Pick Any Battles Carefully

Be careful about the limits or rules you insist on. Have only a certain amount of definite rules for the family, and stick to them. Meanwhile, do not reward arguments by giving them attention 'on demand'. Refuse to get into their little rows, keep away from any power struggles that are going on between siblings. In short, ignore attention-seeking behaviour. Instead, notice their responsible behaviour and praise it, giving attention then. If behaviour needs changing, have a respectful, 'I am unhappy about this' conversation, giving choice on how to change and letting them live with the consequences. Involve the children in decision-making for the family's good. Choose your rules carefully – Is this really important or are you just trying to flex your parental muscles? Making unfair rules only sets a parent up to be inconsistent. If it is not harmful to life or limb or not too socially unacceptable – forget it!

Be Consistent

Be patient, be kind, but be firm and consistent. Put simply, mean what you say, and follow it through each time. Don't change your mind. 'No' today is 'no' tomorrow. By giving in to any pleas, you will make it harder for yourself another day. It gets across a messy message that no rule sticks, and rules can be shifted.

Be Discerning In Your Praise

Words like, 'You are so beautiful' or 'You are so intelligent' are what I call blanket praise and results in your children starting to mistrust and doubt you. 'If I am so clever how did I fail Irish?' A more helpful way of praising is to highlight what a child is doing or has done. 'I love your use of colour in the picture,' 'I like hearing you speak French. Your accent is great.' A child is pleased that they have created something that gives you pleasure. Describing what she has done gives a verbal picture of her own abilities. This empowers her.

Avoid Difficult Situations

There is no shame in avoiding 'hot issues.' Know your child's vulnerable times, like dressing in the morning. Or just after they arrive home from school. Or just as you arrive home from work. Try to avoid conflict at these vulnerable times and ignore or reduce the need for disciplining by anticipating the conflict situation at a time when you're both at a low ebb.

Set A Good Example

Children copy our behaviour. Be a good model to imitate. We cannot be perfect but at least be aware that you are their role model. Good manners and social values need to be taught or modelled by example. Be a good a parent to yourself.

Watch How You Talk To Your Children

Good communication is so important. *Listen* and *talk* things through together. Keep a respectful tone in your voice and keep it friendly. We parents often fall into the trap of our voice getting louder and louder but we do not need to shout to get our message across. The younger the child, the simpler, shorter the sentence. Get onto their eye level and be clear and concise, 'We are leaving now and then we'll go home and have a lovely dinner.' Repeat what you want done again; sometimes, good old repetition works. Often our voice will set the limits for the young. It is not just what we say but how we say it.

How Should We Correct?

We should not need to resort to physical violence. It is not fair or useful for teaching children how to handle difficult emotions or situations. You cannot teach self- discipline by fear – you can only temporarily impose your will.

To correct a child, check you have all the facts, point out what you find wrong with this behaviour, say how you feel about it, and ask for comments from them. Discuss how she could impose limits on herself regarding the behaviour and what she could do about it. Encourage her to think up ideas and consequences for the action herself. Nagging, ordering, scolding and threatening are usually ineffective especially when dealing with the teens. The way forward is through co-operation and dialogue, so that they will eventually become responsible for themselves.

Keeping The Parent/Child Relationship One Of Mutual Respect and Friendship

Yes, teaching self-discipline is a tricky, long drawn out business; getting the balance right is difficult at times. All of us lose our cool, may shout at times, or even slap. If you make a mistake, apologise. If you falter once all is not lost – try again to teach, teach, teach. Don't miss out on being the parent you want to be, giving lots of hugs and kisses and loving words. Everyone, including parents, need them regularly.

WE ARE HAVING MORE PROBLEMS IN OUR FAMILY THESE DAYS

Family Meetings Or Ways Of Improving Family Relations

Today's world is so busy. Many families do not sit and have breakfast around the table any more. Evening meals can be rushed or eaten off a tray in front of the TV. The times when families had the chance for a chat are diminishing. I personally think that this is very sad and that these trends break down the lines of communication between members of the family, harming relationships no end.

Many families may feel that making a contract with another member, or with all of the family, is very strange. Others may feel that making the effort for all the family to meet once a week, say at Sunday breakfast time, to talk about the week, is not a good idea for their family, either.

However, if there are difficulties occurring in family life or there is disharmony or unhappiness in the family, sometimes families may feel it would help to take formal steps to improve the situation for everyone. Perhaps for your particular family an informal meeting, just to say, 'Hi, how's it going' to all the family informally, is a good idea. I like family meetings – they can be fun, refreshing, or angry and frustrating. Whatever they turn out to be, it keeps the door of communication open and gives everyone in the family a chance to air their feelings, be they happy or sad, resentful or thankful.

There is no foolproof recipe for the making of a happy family. But if I had to choose anything that contributes towards making a family happy I would choose, love, communication and co-operation. Having regular times together to chat, share and communicate how we feel and how our life is going is so important. A half an hour spent talking, listening and sharing can turn despondency to hope, sadness into happiness.

There are no definites here. These are just ideas for you to use or not. Some families may like a formal meeting with rules. Others may prefer to keep it just chatting. Here are a few guidelines you could follow should you want to either make a contract with your child or have family meetings. Pick the ones that suit your family to follow.

Making A Contract

RULES – Prior to making a contract, basic rules should be set out.

TIME – Allow a set time for a good discussion, before signing and agreeing a contract.

PURPOSE – Be clear on the purpose of the contract. It is better that the contract only covers one specific behaviour or situation, e.g. Coming home late/ Not fighting with brother John.

IN WRITING – The contract should be put in writing. This will ensure that everyone remembers what was agreed. And it should be dated, with a date for renewal or revaluation given.

SIGNING – The contract should be signed by all concerned. A little picture will do if they cannot write yet.

DISPLAYED – The contract can then be hung in the kitchen on a notice board or wherever you feel is a good spot.

SERIES – As problems occur or situations develop, a series of contracts may be made.

Family Meetings

SCHEDULE – Regular, scheduled meetings can take place at a time agreed with all the family. Work according to the rules agreed on in advance. The family meeting can be formal or informal, taking place at mealtimes or a specified time.

PLAN – If you are starting out on family meetings, it may be a good idea initially to plan it and start with a subject all the family would enjoy, like an outing or holiday.

SHORT – If there are very young children in the family keep the meeting short but the Under 4s can listen in. Alternatively with a young family, instead of a proper family meeting, start with a family time for chatting and playing together, perhaps half an hour 'special family time' once a week.

TOPICS – Before the meeting starts, write down topics of conversations or anything that especially needs to be brought up that week. You might have a blank sheet of paper on the kitchen notice board where ideas can be written down during the week.

LENGTH – Pick a time, place and length for the meeting, perhaps 30 minutes to start with; and not too late because it would be a good idea if they were all in reasonably good humour.

SUSPICION – The teenager may be suspicious of family meetings if you have never tried them before. They may be rebellious and uncooperative at first. Patience may be needed until the teenager learns to trust that the idea is not just another way of you 'telling her what to do!'

SPEAK – There should be no fear in the meetings and people, adults and children alike, should be allowed to speak their piece.

FORMAT – The format could be the topics written down discussed or each family member may take turns in having something to say. Let everybody who wants a turn have a turn, be understanding and listen while others put their point of view across. Easier said than done but try to keep order. Have a rule of no interruptions whilst a person is speaking and agree that no person is allowed more than 5 minutes at a time.

IDEAS – Ask for suggestions on how to deal with situations. When looking for solutions, ask everyone to give their ideas. 'Which do we all feel is the best solution?' Do they all agree to try this? Will they make a commitment to try this for one week? Do they want to make a formal contract? Or just try it out? Try to deal with one issue at a time or it may get confusing.

CHAIRPERSON – Pick a person to 'chair' the meeting each week; they can be leader if things get out of hand. The leader (children and adults taking equal turns) makes sure the topics are dealt with, that the meeting starts and finishes on time.

ASK – Parents should not take over the family meetings, but may need to ask opening questions like, 'What do you mean by that?' or 'So you are saying...' and repeat their suggestions. Ask does everyone feel the same way?

MIXED BAG – Family meeting should not just deal with complaints and problems or they will become a chore. They should include arranging outings, good news, planning holidays or birthdays.

POSITIVE – It is a good idea to end the family meeting on a positive note. For example, if it is held during a meal, bring out their favourite pudding when the meeting is over or give them a special snack, inform them of a surprise visit or just give them a hug.

NOTICE BOARD – Again, any contracts or decisions made can be pinned up on the notice board for all to see through the coming week.

VALUABLE – Family meetings can be valuable in teaching children about teamwork, co-operation, democracy, debate and discussion, and how to be a good listener.

CHAPTER 5

Young Adults –
Dangerous Situations

Our Child Gets Drunk With A Bad Crowd

Working Through Difficult Situations

I feel one of the most important things about alcohol is to educate and inform our children about what alcohol is and what it can do. We tend to take for granted that our children understand about the different strengths of alcohol and all the pros and cons. They don't - so education is the first step. Along with this education is how we parents deal with alcohol ourselves. This will influence our children as well. So before peer pressure starts – and sadly it can start as early as 9-10 years old -- we need to have provided information about alcohol to our children. If you allow the school or their peers to provide this information, you are leaving your child open to experiment and at high risk of getting into trouble. Teenagers like experimenting, are looking for ways to test themselves mentally and physically. They enjoy something that gives them a thrill, however misguided, so talk openly about all aspects of alcohol.

Help Your Child To Say 'No' To Alcohol

- Re-check your own attitude towards alcohol and your own habits. Be a good role model.
- Discuss non-judgementally and in a relaxed way the pros and cons of drinking alcohol, including what happens when you mix alcoholic drinks, for example the fact that spirits are very toxic and when mixed with other drinks like wine can cause over-dosing, sickness, even death.
- Mention the new high-energy drinks and how some people are mixing these with spirits and thus strengthening the toxic effect the alcohol has.
- Let them know that you do not feel the effect straight away and that a person can get drunk without realising it.

- Also discuss how to drink in a more safe way, staying with the one type of drink, eating food with it and drinking slowly.
- Be open to being questioned without being judgmental. Give the facts.
- Explain that drinking alcohol is an activity for adults and that is why it is illegal to sell alcohol to children. Alcohol affects reason and performance, which is why it is illegal for a person to drive when he/she has been drinking. Discuss all this.

Common Sense

SAFE HOME – Know your child's friends and their parents. In a formal or informal way, check out that parents hold the same views as you and want to protect their children from alcohol and drugs. Make a *safe home* pact with the other parents, agreeing to ensure whilst the teenagers are in their home that they will be supervised and it will be an alcohol-free zone.

CONTACT – Know where your children are and let them know where you are. Have a line of contact.

DECISION – Take a firm decision on alcohol and drugs so that your children understand the importance of any decisions they make.

BE AWARE – Be aware when young people are home or come home at night. Stay alert or ask to be wakened.

LIFT – Let your children know that you are there for them and if they are in difficulties, whatever the time or place, they can telephone you for help or a lift home.

CHECK – Telephone to check with the parents or dance, disco or party, to verify what the activity is? Is it supervised? Will alcohol be available?

LATE TIMES – At family meetings, discuss reasonable home times or special late times for coming home at weekdays, weekends and holiday times, too.

HOSTS – If you are the hosts of a party, be visible, know who is there and what is going on. Do not allow gate crashers or potential harmful activities.

INFORM – If you ever find alcohol on a child or a child drunk, inform his/her parent immediately and protect the child until the parent arrives.

Be Aware
Children tend to get alcohol from:–
— the drinks cabinet in their own home or
— by asking someone older to buy it for them.

They tend to drink alcohol:–
— before going into dances, disco, or parties;
— when parents are not at home;
— before and after football games;
— congregating around shop corners;
— house hopping or in another part of the house when their parents may be drinking or entertaining at the same time.

Why Do Children Drink Alcohol?
• Simply out of curiosity to see what happens and what it's like.
• Peer pressure.
• Because it's available.
• Escapism, especially if experiencing any problems at home or school.
• Rebelling against 'home rules'.
• Boredom or over-indulgent or inattentive parents.
• They may have poor role models.

Teenage Parties – Your Party

1. Discuss the rules and plan the party, with definite start and end times, and see the guest list well in advance.
2. Rules could include no alcohol, no smoking, no leaving then returning, no gate crashers, lights on at all times, specific places that are off limits.
3. Accept the responsibility of having the party - be aware and alert.
4. Perhaps have another parent to help you and also have fun with. When the parents drop the children off, make sure they all have the phone number and know the collection time and if you want to, get their number also.

Your Teen Going To A Party

1. Verify that parental supervision will be in place, and no alcohol etc., allowed.
2. Know the address and phone number of the party. Introduce yourself to the host family and wait to see your child inside the house.
3. Make sure your child knows that she can telephone you at any time should a difficulty arise.
4. Make sure your child knows never to get into a car when the person who is driving has been drinking.
5. Be awake to welcome your child home.

Signs And Symptoms Of Alcohol Abuse

*   Personality changes, such as lack of motivation. Irritability and mood swings.
*   Physical changes if addicted, such as unkempt appearance and changes in sleeping or eating patterns.
*   Behavioural changes, like lack of school attendance. Not doing well with school work, lying, tantrums over little things.

REMEMBER ... With alcohol, PREVENTION is best, but if your child makes a mistake once discuss, in a non-judgmental way, the consequences if it happens again. Discuss all aspects and let her know that if she does it again she will have to live with the consequences ... and what these consequences are. Keep your tone respectful, but be sure she knows that you will stand firm on this issue as a way of protecting her.

See Handling Difficult Situations (p. 140) and Working Out Compromises (see p. 99) for guidelines on dealing with the discussions. As with all teenager situations, keep the talk friendly and the communications lines open.

Start off by encouraging her to talk about why she wants or needs to drink. How does she view drinking alcohol? Listen to her opinions and repeat what she says back to her to make sure you have her ideas correctly then tell her yours. In a warm manner, tell her of your fears about alcohol, how it can lead to irresponsible behaviour, reckless driving, casual sex and untold heartache. Ask her can she understand your concerns and what she thinks about them. Once each side is clearer as to how the other feels, are there compromises that can be reached, rules that can be kept by both sides? Can you agree on a plan or set of rules about drinking, for example not more than two pints, never drinking and driving etc.? Talk about it together and make an agreement to suit you all.

OUR DAUGHTER NEARLY HAD A CRASH BECAUSE OF RECKLESS DRIVING. I AM NOT EVEN SURE IF SHE HAD BEEN DRINKING

Teaching Responsibility

Here we have the problem where we parents love our children and they put themselves into dangerous situations that we can see clearly and they don't. Naturally we get very upset, not to say frightened for them and enraged at their reckless irresponsibility.

So how do we react? Well, we may shout, argue, threaten, scold, even feel like slapping our child. Sadly this only upsets everyone concerned and is not effective in getting a child to face her responsibility. In fact, it may build a barrier between parent and child, driving them apart. Yes, we may be furious and upset but shouting will not help matters. What can we do?

This could be a life and death situation so we must effectively and sensibly make sure the child knows the danger she has placed herself and others in – yes, a discussion and firm action needs to be taken but it must be in a way that the child feels she has taken the responsible steps herself, so that she is not just willing to be responsible just when you are there, but will do the right, safe thing for herself and others at all times.

Dealing With Difficult Situations And Teaching Responsibility

WAIT – for a suitable time to discuss the situation, not when either of you are angry or upset, but when you are both calm. If necessary, take a shower or a walk to relax. Postpone the talk but let her know you are genuinely interested in listening to her.

HER POINT OF VIEW – Ask her about her point of view on the situation. Did she feel she was driving dangerously? Does she feel that it is wrong to drink and drive? Why? LISTEN carefully, repeat what she says to make sure you have her ideas correctly. Ask, 'Do I understand you clearly?' and repeat. What makes her feel that? Let her express her views without comment so she can speak freely and so that you really understand where she is coming from. Take your time with this stage, otherwise you will not grasp the root of the problem. Young adults will listen to you more readily if you have listened to them.

YOUR POINT OF VIEW – Explain what you think about the situation, again not saying 'You' but 'I.' For example, 'I am frightened that one day you'll crash the car, hurting or killing yourself or some innocent bystander.' Explain your difficulties with what she has said. Point out your own values and what you feel is acceptable behaviour. Be honest about your feelings deep inside, your fears, your hopes and your moral standards. Talking in this way makes you vulnerable but avoids blame and wins respect and hopefully co-operation. Ask her to respond to what you have said. Does she understand your point of view? Does she know why, as a parent, you cannot allow her to behave in this way?

WAY FORWARD – Together you can decide on the way forward. Is there a way together she could agree to keep herself and others safe? What would happen if? How could we improve things? What agreement would please us both and keep everyone safe? Encourage her to come up with the details.

PLAN – When the agreement is made, weigh up the pros and cons to it. Then write down the plan, including the rules of what, where and how! For example, suggest one month's rest from using the car. Never drink and drive. Only use the car in the daytime – or whatever you decide between you. Perhaps agree to review the situation in one week or month's time and don't forget the consequences that will happen if the agreement is broken.

CONSEQUENCES – Instead of punishing for reckless behaviour, place the emphasis on letting the teenager learn by the consequences of her own actions. Because she drove in a careless way and endangered her own and others lives, she is not allowed to have the car for one month. Over that time the LISTENING, DISCUSSION and AGREEMENT PLAN is worked out in a friendly way until all concerned are in agreement.

BROKEN – If the agreement is ever broken, the consequences discussed in the agreement are put into action. For example, no car for one month. Let her know in a discussion how disappointed you are that the plan did not work, but also that you are relieved that they are alive and no one else was hurt. Perhaps, after one minor set back, the plan can work and we could all try again?

RESPONSIBILITY – Be firm about her having to live with the discussed consequences in the plan. Then discuss the plan again and why it failed. During these discussions, emphasise your hope that this is a minor slip but that the more times she proves she is not responsible then the ultimate consequence would be that you would be too afraid to let her have the car at all, to protect her and others. Does she understand you feeling this way? Work at encouraging responsibility.

MY CHILD STOLE FROM THE LOCAL SHOP. I WAS SO EMBARRASSED. HOW SHOULD I PUNISH HER?

I have written many times about letting our children learn from the consequences of their own actions. Here is such a situation. It is very hard to let your child suffer the consequences in this case. The loving parent may be tempted not to tell the shop or the authorities that their child has stolen something. Yet this is the very action that may lead her never to do anything like it again.

What To Do

Firstly, pick an appropriate time as previously mentioned and *calmly* ask why she stole the item? Listen carefully. Was she encouraged by peers? Was it just to see what happened? Was it that she wanted the object so badly? How does she feel about it now? What does she generally feel about stealing? This is a very important question – these days our moral lines get very hazy when some people seem to get away with a certain type of stealing and do not get punished. It could lead to a good discussion. But at the end of the day, is it right for people to be able to steal?

Listen. Let her explain fully. Don't rush her and *check all the facts* concerned.

Then say how you feel about the situation and *why* the behaviour was wrong. You may challenge her behaviour and say why it was wrong but try not to scold or preach. Ask questions and let her answer them, so it is not you just moralising.

Discuss what action you feel you need to take. This may be very varied, depending on why and how and what the teenager stole. It could range from being grounded to giving the amount the item cost to charity, or to more severe action. Discuss why you are taking the action you feel you must take and be open!

Here are some examples of the more severe action you may consider taking:–

- You could take the item back to the shop and make your child apologise and return the item.
- You could take her back to the shop and make her give her pocket money every week until the object is paid for.
- If you know the shop owner well, you may even ask would he/she trust your child to work in the shop to pay for the cost of the item involved.
- Or you may decide the stealing was serious enough to tell the police, explaining that your reasons for doing so is to teach her to take responsibility for her actions and prevent recurrence. Discuss this with the police also and they may be very understanding.

By working together with the shop or authority involved, you may come up with a plan that would positively teach your child and encourage good behaviour, with no return to theft.

This might involve working in a voluntary way for the good of the community.

It is very difficult not to rescue our teenagers from their own follies but it can be a very effective way of encouraging self-discipline. Remember our goal is to encourage the teen to become responsible for herself and for others in society, hopefully making a good caring person for the world.

Use the guidelines from previous questions Working Out Compromises (p. 99) and Handling Difficult Situations (p. 140) if you need extra advice on how to handle these discussions.

Keep friendly and respectful throughout – it is her behaviour you did not like, not her. End with a positive note to encourage the right behaviour. Remember there is no need for scolding; stay friendly. Lean towards co-operation instead of thinking on the lines of punishment. Think in terms of discussion, with both of you giving your side of the story. Give the, 'I cannot allow' message, pointing out the natural or applied consequences of her actions.

Keep faith with your child, think the best of her, deal with her honestly and truthfully and it will pay dividends. Emphasise positive direction, use re-direction rather than inhibition. Take more of an interest in her life and in what positive things she is or could be doing.

Strive for the non-punishment approach. Being blamed or punished makes self-esteem fail. Think of ways to help her learn the right way to behave and practise self-discipline rather than ways to make her suffer for the wrong she has done.

I THINK MY DAUGHTER MAY BE TAKING DRUGS AND I DON'T KNOW WHAT TO DO

Q

Signs And Management Of Drug Taking

Most parents have the horrors about even the thought of their precious child taking drugs. But in the world today, the availability of drugs is all around us and they can be made so tempting. The reasons for taking them are the same as for alcohol – curiosity, peer pressure, insecurity for whatever reason, boredom, thrills, escape, rebelling against authority, being brought up in affluence without enough parental control, low self-esteem, poor role models or perhaps even the parents take drugs.

Signs And Symptoms Of Drug Taking

Any normal teenager can have some of the behavioural problems noted. It is if they have a few of the symptoms and you instinctively feel as a parent something is wrong, that there may be an underlying drug problem. These can include:–

- *Personality changes*, such as less caring, lack of motivation, irritability, mood swings from euphoria to depression.
- *Physical changes*, such as letting herself go, weight loss, pale, circles under the eyes, low resistance to infections, change in sleeping and eating patterns (like binge eating and sleeping odd hours).
- *Behavioural Changes*, such as not attending school, lack of interest in schoolwork or job, always wanting money or money going missing, new friends that just appear and disappear no surnames known, lying, secretiveness, lack of concentration, spending more time away from home.
- *Physical Evidence*, such as smoking and use rolling papers, using mouthwashes, odd objects like roach clips, pipes, the use of incense to disguise smells, marks on arms.

What To Do If You Suspect Your Child Is Taking Drugs

Again, remember that PREVENTION IS BETTER THAN CURE. Follow the *safe home* policy…
- Know where your child is, who her friends are and if the parents have the same idea on parental guidance as you.
- Know where your child is and that she know where you can be contacted at all times.

- Educate her about the dangers of drugs
- Be aware, keep the lines of communication open with your child, let her know you can always be phoned for help, a ride or if ever she is in difficulties.
- Always verify that venues for parties, sleepovers or discos are places without drugs, alcohol etc.

If You Suspect Any Child Of Being High On Drugs...

1. Stay calm.
2. Try to find out what she has taken, how much, when and how.
3. Contact a doctor, and the hospital accident and emergency department, or the Poisons Centre, if child in any way ill or incoherent.
4. If it is not your child, contact her parent.
5. If it is your child there is no point in having a discussion whilst she is high. Let her know that you will discuss the problem first thing in the morning.
6. Put her to bed and check her physical condition regularly through the night.
7. Please do not shout, criticise or be verbally abusive to your child. There is no point. I understand that you are frightened for her, hurt and angry. But it is a waste of time and emotion.

Management Of A Child Taking Drugs

Before the discussion make her clean up any mess she has made – if she wets the bed she changes it, if she's been sick, she clears it up and washes any dirty clothes.

Then quietly sit down and have a discussion, pick the time carefully when all is calm. Start with her explaining where she got the drugs, from whom and all the circumstances. This will take time, encouragement, and probing questions. Do it in the tender tone, in a non-aggressive way. It is because you love her and care about her that you need to know how to help her. Listen to her carefully – it will help you understand how it happened. Once you have listen for some time and let her have her complete say, it is your turn.

Explain your feeling, saying, 'I cannot accept this behaviour, it is dangerous and can hurt even kill you. A parent's job is to protect etc.' Explain that the consequence of her actions are that you will be monitoring her movements and life much more closely to protect her. Also discuss the steps you will need to take to do this. Ask questions and get her input, but be *firm*. Establish an agreement about future behaviour, which may be something like this:–

- Grounded for a period of time.
- That you will know where she is at all times and will verify this with the parents or places concerned.
- Agree on a reasonable HOME TIME for weekends and weekdays.
- Agree that there will be no further experimenting with DRUGS or ALCOHOL and you expect 100% compliance; if the agreement is broken then stricter rules will become enforced as a consequence of her actions.

Next...

LYING – Do not be fooled. Clever lying or deception is a feature of these situations. Do not simply be fooled by a tearful promise that she will stop. Do not hide the incident from other members of the family. Do not cover for her but let the consequences of her actions be known.

ACTIVITIES – Try to think of ways and other activities that may encourage her away from drugs and from the places where she may be tempted to take them again.

MAJOR PROBLEM – Discuss with your partner, counsellors, teachers or health professional if you think your daughter has a major drug problem. There are schemes and places especially there to help children come off drugs so find your local help agency. Getting help any way you can from local youth agencies, priest, rabbi, doctor, guidance counsellors – anywhere!

TOUGH LOVE – If a child has taken drugs what she needs most is help and loving support. Not condemnation. But she needs *tough love* as well, and that involves you being there to support but being consistent in your rules and agreements.

MYTHS – Make sure that your child is fully educated to the dangers, pros and cons of drug taking. Dispel any myths like, 'It does not harm' or 'Everyone's doing it.'

REFUSAL SKILLS – Teach her how to say NO to drugs. Teach refusal skills; if necessary role-play what she would do if (a) so called 'friends' were urging her to take drugs or (b) a dealer offered some. Teach delay tactics, or how they could get out of the situation safely.

EXCHANGING VIEWS – Remember that caring parenting, discussion and the respectful exchanging of views of all parties involved, are much more effective in helping a child not to take drugs in the first place and keeping off drugs in the future.

I HAVE TALKED TO MY DAUGHTER ABOUT THE FACTS OF LIFE, SO SHE UNDERSTANDS ABOUT SEX, BUT NOW SHE HAS A STEADY BOYFRIEND. I AM TERRIFIED OF HER GETTING PREGNANT

Q

There is no right time to talk about sex. The facts of life should be talked about as a normal part of life. When a child is young and sees a pregnant woman, you can simply explain how the baby grows inside her body. This leads naturally to the question, 'How does it gets there?' Daddy has the seed and Mummy has the egg. They come out when having sex or making love; when the egg and the seed meet, it starts to develop into a baby.

When a child is young, keep the answers simple and honest. As they grow older the questions will get more complicated but always just answer as simply and honestly as you can. If you don't know the answer, look it up together or if it embarrasses you, say so.

Sex And Sexuality

Don't let your daughter get the information from just her friends because there are many myths and legends about sex that are just not true. Ensure she knows the straight facts about sex.

During this book I have tried to emphasise the importance of keeping communication lines open, talking respectfully and openly about all things. Sex is a very sensitive issue and a personal one. But if you have a good relationship with your daughter it should be OK for you to enquire how she feels with relation to sex.

Well before a girl starts to have body changes and begin menstruation, sex and attitudes towards sex should be discussed frankly and openly. Use everyday life opportunities to discuss the dangers and joys of having sex.

Sex can be lovely when two people are in love and mutually respect each other. However, before anyone has sex they must consider the potential DANGER involved. It can be discussed openly at a family meeting but it should also be discussed on a one-to-one private basis, too. When talking about sex be sensitive, non-judgmental, and do not preach. Talk in an interested way. *Ask questions and listen.* Find out what and how much she knows by asking, 'Do you understand that?' or 'What does that mean to you?'

The dangers of having sex are...

(1) Unwanted pregnancy.

(2) Diseases that are sexually transmitted; one called AIDS can even cause death.

(3) It can leave you vulnerable if someone has sex with you for the wrong reasons.

Long before a person starts dating, these issues should be brought into the open and discussed frankly in the home. Before your daughter considers having sex, she needs to have thought all these matters through.

COMFORTABLE – Explain that if a person is not comfortable talking about sex and birth control with their boyfriend or girl friend, then they are not ready to have sex. Because if they are not ready to take the responsibility for protecting themselves from pregnancy and diseases, they are not ready to have sex.

SEXUAL HEALTH – If a couple is thinking about being sexually active they should fully understand the facts about sexual health. That is where the parent comes in. Don't expect such important information about sexual health and attitudes to be left to school or other people. Ensure that your child has the facts about sex, plus your views on sex and sexual behaviour.

FEELINGS – Do not leave talking about sex until she is walking out the door on her first date. Well before this, be assured she has the straight facts and has worked out her own feelings on the issues, and that you know what her and your feelings are.

Some Misconceptions

Here are a few 'misconceptions' about sex. You could use them as a base to *start discussions* with your children. Listen to what they say and how they react.

- You can't get pregnant the first time. *Wrong.*
- I'd be able to tell if my boyfriend had a disease. *Wrong*
- The boy just has to withdraw his penis and the girl won't get pregnant. *Wrong*
  The lubricating sperm, even prior to the come, has sperm in it that can make you pregnant and withdrawal is difficult to get right, anyway.
- Using birth control takes away the romance. *Wrong*
  Using birth control does not take away the enjoyment or romance. Instead it can help you relax and enjoy sex without the worry of an unwanted pregnancy.
- Birth control is the female's responsibility. *Wrong*
  Both partners can get disease. But also, in a loving, mutually respectful relationship, both partners should share the responsibility, and trust and care for each other.

Sometimes girls can be urged or encouraged to have sex without being fully ready for the responsibility. DISCUSS with your daughter how she feels about situations like these...

Q. What if a partner says, 'If you loved me, you'd have sex with me!'
A. 'If you loved me, you wouldn't pressure me to do something I am not ready to do yet or I do not feel comfortable doing.'

Q. You are not a real man/woman if you have not had sex!
A. Sex does not make you a man or a woman, it's what you are inside that counts.

Q. Everyone does it.
A. I am not everyone – I am me.

Q. What are you waiting for? There is something wrong with you!

A. I am waiting until it is the right choice for me. There is nothing wrong with me; perhaps there is something wrong with you.

Q. I am tired of waiting for you to make your mind up.
A. I am tired of being pressurised.

Q What are you afraid of?
A. I am not afraid. I am just not ready.

Q. Are you going to sleep with me or am I just wasting my time on you?
A. If that is all you care about, yes, you are wasting your time and mine.

Q. If you don't sleep with me, I'll find someone who will!
A. See you later.

These are just some ways of saying 'no' to sex if a person is not ready. Talk about them. And discuss other ways a person can put pressure on another to have sex. Don't be afraid to have a good laugh sometimes when discussing these issues; they are important but we should never lose our sense of humour. When our family had a discussion about sex, I fell about the place laughing at some things my children said.

We as parents need to talk openly about sex with our children so they can develop a healthy attitude towards sex, sexuality and the opposite sex. Let them know how you feel about sex and sexual standards, without preaching. Perhaps you feel casual sex tends to cheapen a person. That if a person 'sleeps around', they are not showing respect for themselves or anyone else. Or perhaps if a person uses safe sex you feel free love is fine between consenting adults. Let them know about your views and how you feel. Explain that you hope they will feel the same way but you can't make them, only advise and hope for co-operation. Listen to how they feel about it all and have an open, non-judgemental discussion.

This book is all about how we, as parents, teach our children to take responsibility for themselves and respect others. Teaching good sexual conduct is just a follow on from this. Our values should be given in a non-judgmental way but it is common sense to have sex with someone…

1.   Who we know well.
2.   Who we can be sure is healthy.
3.   Who we really care about and ideally love and are committed to in a special way.

While explaining our values, we should also let it be known that sex is much more than a physical act, no matter how enjoyable, and is much better as part of a caring, sharing long-term partnership.

Remember as you are discussing these matters, that your child is forming his/her own values about sex so be honest, truthful and *Listen* more than you talk. Asking sensitive personal questions may not encourage a child to speak. Instead, ask indirect questions that do not put them on the spot, like, 'What advice would you give a young brother before his first date?' or 'What if a girl or fella kisses and cuddles and gets carried away?'

You may talk about your past, your first love. Make it fun. Was he a big drip? Always let your children know that you are there for them even if they make a mistake and that you will always support them.

Encourage all friends, including those of the opposite sex, to visit and be made welcome in your home. Let them know you are happy to have a caring loving, friendly, home where all are welcome. That way you'll be around when friendships are developing and will be able to guide them in any developing relationship.

MY TEENAGE SON SEEMS TO BE VERY DOWN LATELY AND YOU HEAR ALL THESE STORIES ABOUT DEPRESSED TEENAGERS COMMITTING SUICIDE. I DON'T WANT TO OVERREACT BUT WHAT SHOULD I BE DOING TO HELP HIM?

Q

Recognising and Coping With Depression

The word depression is used in many ways and can have many meanings. Low moods and feeling unhappy at times is normal, it is our reaction to the losses and disappointments that life may throw at us. However, such despondency should be short-lived. If this sadness becomes overwhelming, continues over a longer period or has no apparent reason, then it is time to take steps to help.

Depression can creep up on a person and sometimes it is a family member or friend who actually recognises that there is a problem. Being depressed can go hand in hand with other symptoms such as tiredness, sleeping problems, feeling run down, mood swings, loss of appetite and withdrawal. Some may turn to alcohol, cigarettes or drugs because they cannot cope and this only makes the problem worse.

So what can we do to help if we feel that someone close to us is depressed? First of all, simply ensure that he is getting a healthy, wholesome diet, eating regular meals, getting enough exercise and having a healthy sleep pattern. Stressful situations should be avoided if possible. Sometimes sad people can bottle things up, so take the time to sit down and ask why he seems sad, is anything worrying him, can you help in any way at all? LISTEN CAREFULLY. It is not helpful to tell him to snap out of it or give a lecture. Activity is important; keep him occupied with constructive tasks so that he is not lying around focusing on his negative thoughts.

If, having taken these steps, you feel that your son is

depressed – and remember, you know him so well – then talk to him about seeking help. The first step is usually an appointment with your G.P. He may be reluctant to do this but with a little encouragement and if you accompany him, he may be relieved that someone is making the decision for him. Both of you should think clearly about what you are going to say to your G.P. so if necessary, write down the symptoms that he is feeling and the things that you have noticed happening yourself.

It will then be up to your G.P. to assess the situation and pick the appropriate treatment, for example anti-depressants, psychotherapy or counselling. If, however, you are still unsure about what action you should take, remember that there are others who may support and guide you. Talk in confidence to a friend or family member, the minister of your church, or even a voluntary body such as Aware or the Samaritans.

Be supportive, positive and a good listener. Depression is a temporary illness that can be overcome.

"He needs to work on his eye-hand co-ordination, but for a month old he really looks a runner for Áras an Uachtarán."

CHAPTER 6

Conclusion

AS PARENTS, WE SHOULD ASK OURSELVES REGULARLY WHAT WE REALLY WANT FOR OUR CHILDREN.

Do we want them to be good children? If so what does that mean? Children are not born 'good' or 'bad'. A good character takes times and effort to develop. Experiences and the way they are treated by their parents and the world help mould children into the characters that they ultimately become. It is said that the basic character of a child is there by the age of 10 years. This suggests that we parents have a major role in developing our children's character.

This is both a huge responsibility and great honour. Imagine this unique, wonderful human being can be moulded like a beautiful crystal. Yes, the environment and inside genes and outside influences all have a part to play. But that is a small part compared to the tremendous influence we can have as parents.

It is a great challenge to be a parent. Imagine you have the power to be *the parent you want to be*, the parent perhaps you wanted to have or were lucky enough to have yourself.

There is no doubt that a good character develops when a child feels loved, approved of, wanted, trusted and accepted for just who they are. A child brought up in a loving atmosphere that encourages independence, self-discipline and is consistent with its principles and values will thrive. A child with a good character is happy and secure, has consideration for others, is fair in their dealings with others, and makes the most of what life brings them.

One way of ensuring that our children are given the right influences is by being a 'good parent' to *ourselves*. We are the example, the constant model to copy. We should try to be the way we would want our children to see us.

So this poses another big question – Are we making the

162

most of our lives? Are we following the PRINCIPLES that we believe in?

- Be a good example. Be a positive parent; provide your children with a person who knows how to enjoy life. Your goal, in a sense, is to teach your children to become their own parents and take over where you left off.

- Think about the parent you want to be, explore the reasons why. Take up the challenge. Imagine a world of loving parents, living the happy life they wanted. Raising caring, happy, self-disciplined, fulfilled children.

- Value yourself as a parent and as a person. Treat your children with respect and they will value themselves too.

Through this book I have aimed at helping you create a family of values and principles. Teaching the right way to behave by discussion, example, communication and consequences in an atmosphere of mutual respect. Before I finish the book I will just write a few more ideas or suggestions to exercise your mind. Good parenting does not come naturally to us all. We have to learn, question and try out different ideas to find which methods suit our particular family. So I leave you with these thoughts.

- Take your parenting *seriously*. These are the people of the world you are raising – the world is relying on you to do a good job.

- Be a good example they can model themselves on.

- Respect your children as you would others, talk to them in a loving way. Children value themselves the way they are valued.

- Let them know they are loved unconditionally, in actions and words, regularly.

- *Talk* and *listen* to your child often.

- Provide clear limits for acceptable behaviour and *be consistent*.

- *Praise* often. Find something positive to say about them daily.

- Offer them *choices* so that they have opportunities to develop self-discipline and independence.

- *Keep your sense of humour* and keep things in the right perspective. There is nothing so binding in a relationship, family, or friendship as a good laugh.

- Don't feel you are too old to change your ways. Change for the good what you can and learn to live with what you can't change.

- Be as healthy, happy and as fulfilled as you can be for yourself, treating all others with a caring respect. This will guide your children to be same. So look after yourselves and your children, and have as good a life as you can for your children and yourself.

You have a great privilege. Enjoy parenting – the world awaits your success!

Books That May Help You

Learning Problems
Lost for Words by Wyn McCormack (Tower Press)

Teens
Help! For parents of teenagers by J.I. Clarke (HarperCollins)
Help Yourself for Teens by Dave Peter (Penguin)

Death
FOR THE VERY YOUNG:
On The Wings of a Butterfly by M. Maple (Parenting Press, Seattle)

Older Children
How it feels when a parent dies by Jill Krementz (Gollancz)

Teens
Straight talk about death for teenagers by Earl A. Grollman (Beacon Press. Boston)

Others
The Step-Parent's Parachute by Flora McEvedy (Time Warner)

The Sensory-Sensitive Child by Karen A. Smith & Karen R. Gouze (HarperCollins)

Useful Telephone Numbers and Websites

ASSOCIATION OF CHILDREN IN HOSPITAL 061-314111
www.each-for-sick-children.org

AIM Family Services   01-6708363
www.aimfamilyservices.ie

AL-ANON ALATEEN Family Groups, 01-6708363 or 01-8732699 (Dublin) / 021 4311899 (Cork)
www.al-anon.org

ATTENTION DEFICIT HYPER-ACTIVITY DISORDER
www.adhdireland.com

AWARE (depression support) 1890 303302
www.aware.ie

BARNARDOS National Office and General Queries
01-4530355
www.barnardos.ie

BARNADOS / SOLÁS – Bereavement Counselling Service for Children confidential helpline (Monday-Friday 10am – 12pm) 01-4732110

BODYWHYS (support for anorexia / bulimia nervosa)
1890 200444
www.bodywhys.ie

CARI (for children and families affected by sexual abuse)
1890 924567
www..cari.ie

CHERISH Association of Single Parents
2 Lr. Pembroke St., Dublin 2 Tel: 01-6629212,
Info Line: 1890 66 22 12

CHILDLINE (ISPCC) 1800 666666
www.ispcc.ie

CHILDMINDING IRELAND (support and information for
childminders and parents) 0404-64007

CURA (Pregnancy Counselling Service) 1850 622626
www.cura.ie

DEPARTMENT OF SOCIAL AND FAMILY AFFAIRS,
Aras Mhic Dhiarmada, Store St., Dublin 1.
01-8748444

DRUGS/HIV Helpline 1800 459459
(Confidential support and information to addicted teens,
pressured teens or worried parents)
www.dap.ie

GAY SWITCHBOARD DUBLIN (parents support)
01-8721055
www.gayswitchboard.ie

LALECHE LEAGUE (information on breastfeeding),
St Patrick's Lodge, Summerhill Rd., Dunboyne, Co. Meath.
01 8251798
www.lalecheleague.org

LIFE PREGNANCY COUNSELLING SERVICE
30 Dame Street, Dublin 2
01-679 0694 National Helpline: 1850 28 12 81

NATIONAL CHILDBIRTH TRUST
32 Lr. O'Connell St., Dublin 1 01-8747247

PARENTLINE, Helpline/ Parents Under Stress, Carmichael
House, North Brunswick Street, Dublin 7 0808 800 2222
www.parentline.ie

PARENTS ALONE SUPPORT SERVICE 01 864 1964
Help with crisis pregnancy and young one-parent families
www.dublin.ie / parentsalone

PARENTS: DRUGS AWARENESS
The Red House, Clonliffe College, Dublin 3.
01-8360911
www.dap.ie

PARENTS EQUALITY   Shared Parenting and Joint Custody
Association, Clanbrassil Street, Dundalk, Co. Louth
042-933 3163
www.parentalequality.ie

SAMARITANS   1850 6090901
www.samaritans.org

WELLWOMAN CENTRE, 35 Lower Liffey St., Dublin 1.
01-872 8051
www.wellwomancentre.ie

Index